"*Citizen King* is a *Chicken Soup*, *The Secret*, *Three Feet from Gold*, *Outwitting the Devil*, reader 'must have.' Some books are for the head. Some are for the heart. Others are for entertainment. And a few, a very few, pierce the soul. I recommend that all of my readers, and famous publication fans, read Les Jensen's *Citizen King* as a cell phone recharge to full bars for your spirit and soul. While reading this book, you will experience the pure joy that your spirit desires, and deserves!"

—Berny Dohrmann, Chairman,
CEO SPACE INTERNATIONAL

"Les Jensen's zeal and excitement fill these pages with empowerment. In his new book, *Citizen King: The New Age of Power*, you'll discover amazing strategies for dissolving boundaries blocking your power. You'll learn about the amazing power of acceptance in dispelling negative tendencies. With the help of this book you'll be able to find that deep state of joy and satisfaction. Please don't miss this amazing book!"

—Peter Ragnar, author of *Finding Heart: How to Live with Courage in a Confusing World*

# CITIZEN
# KING

## The New Age of *Power*

LES JENSEN

**BALBOA.**
PRESS

A DIVISION OF HAY HOUSE

Balboa Press books may be ordered through booksellers or by contacting:

Balboa Press
A Division of Hay House
1663 Liberty Drive
Bloomington, IN 47403
www.balboapress.com
1 (877) 407-4847

Because of the dynamic nature of the Internet, any web addresses or
links contained in this book may have changed since publication and
may no longer be valid. The views expressed in this work are solely those
of the author and do not necessarily reflect the views of the publisher,
and the publisher hereby disclaims any responsibility for them.

The author of this book does not dispense medical advice or prescribe the
use of any technique as a form of treatment for physical, emotional, or medical
problems without the advice of a physician, either directly or indirectly. The
intent of the author is only to offer information of a general nature to help you
in your quest for emotional and spiritual well-being. In the event you use any
of the information in this book for yourself, which is your constitutional right,
the author and the publisher assume no responsibility for your actions.

Any people depicted in stock imagery provided by Thinkstock are
models, and such images are being used for illustrative purposes only.
Certain stock imagery © Thinkstock.

Print information available on the last page.

ISBN: 978-1-5043-3503-4 (sc)
ISBN: 978-1-5043-3505-8 (hc)
ISBN: 978-1-5043-3504-1 (e)

Balboa Press rev. date: 06/29/2015

# CONTENTS

\*

# PREFACE

We all are made from the same fabric, a vibrant and endless point of human consciousness. We all are the thing itself. Consciousness incarnate. We all have a body and our own unique personality. And we all have that inner place where our own crafted inspiration flows when nurtured.

When we get clear that the infinite creative opportunity of the moment is fulfilled through the portals of the *heart* and the *soul*, a much bigger outcome becomes possible. It is for those individuals who can walk intuitively in that moment that all possibilities actually do become possible. That creative dialogue has been operating forever, under the language of energy interacting with itself.

You are that energy now. You are a projector, projecting the movie of your life onto the screen, able to embody any story of your choosing. To trust your intuition, and to follow the inspiration of the moment, allows you to become free. Genuinely free. And there is immense peace there too. You become comfortable living your own life, without hesitation or second thought. *Pure authentic you.*

Trust in *your dream* as being the best seat in the house. Trust in the vision of what *your* life would look like if you were to follow your dreams without hesitation, of what your life could look like if you were to only live from a place of joy. Trust in *that* vision for your life, and the world will reflect back an incredible journey for you to live out.

That is the arena of the Citizen King.
That is the arena of *you* living *your* life as a Citizen King.

The infinite potential of our human nature never dims.

\*

# ACKNOWLEDGMENTS

Where do I begin? So many people touch us in remarkable ways. So many people have deeply touched me in my own life. To my kids, know that you are loved. Enjoy your own personal sovereignty. Dream your best dream as you choose. To Gretchen, who has shown me what unconditional love looks like. To Robyn too. What a road we have traveled. To Susan Westfall, my editor, thank you for walking this journey with me. I so appreciate how your thoughts and insights have improved this book. Thank you for all of your support through the birthing of this book. To my siblings, you know who you are. To the people who pushed me in all the right ways, I love where I have landed, and I thank you!

To absolute freedom and untethered
sovereignty to every human on this planet!
To Heaven on Earth!

# Chapter 1

# TO BE A KING ...

The lights come down. The theater is filled to capacity. The movie is about to start. You settle in, getting comfortable in your seat, as you anticipate the wonderful story that is about to begin. It is the story of the life of a *king*. This story starts in the 1800's, not that long ago. It was a time when we had a clear idea of what being a king was all about. The old idea of a king as a person empowered to choose whatever he wanted. The king had no one to challenge his authority. He had the authority to take actions on his own, having dominion over others. However, the *Citizen King* concept of being a king is quite different than the stories of yore, for it is really the story of mastering the possibilities of life itself—a personal triumph of sorts. But before we go down that road and embark upon this path, let's bring to the discussion the concept of this budding king—the *king* that is in *you* now.

The notion of being a king is really not a new idea. We have had kings ruling the culture of humanity from as far back as we can remember. But there's a new idea of being a king that brings to the screen an exciting and powerful idea of what our future can be.

In the past, the idea of being a king involved a single person having dominion over a single kingdom, with one king ruling over the masses, the culture, and the destiny of the kingdom. But to allow a single person to have such sway over so many people no longer fits the healthy idea of what it means to be an empowered human being. For all of us to be able to experience what it genuinely means to fulfill our own immense personal potential, without tether or restraint, is to know what it means to embody the idea of being a king in our own kingdom. It is the idea of achieving a state of absolute personal sovereignty to create an empowered vision that can flow freely from your own *heart* and *soul*.

To be a healthy king is to engage your potential. It is to honor your heart and soul's vision for what *your* life can be. To totally honor the vision of your soul, is to learn how to fulfill your potential in each passing moment of every single day. That is the endgame for mastering your true power, a place of healthy and balanced human consciousness for which humanity has been searching.

This new idea of being a king, a personal king, an individual king, a *Citizen King*, brings to the screen an idea of the future that truly has no limits, a vision of our lives that has no boundaries. It holds so much raw potential that has never been totally fulfilled by humanity, yet here we sit at the doorway to the future with the idea of the king, and the idea of the kingdom, that can make this new idea possible. The idea that each one of us is a *citizen* too. We can all personify our own authentic vision or *dream* of what our lives could look like, and to do that would create our own personal Heaven on Earth.

Citizen King, the idea of it, is really a very powerful concept, because human consciousness is very powerful, the most powerful substance on the planet. Everything man has ever created has started as an idea in the mind of human consciousness, just like your consciousness now.

You are human consciousness personified. And held within that infinite field of potential is the vision of *your* life that *your* soul has had from the time of *your* birth, to be created on your own screen, to create any storyline you can envision. It is from this infinite field of potential that anything becomes possible in your life.

# Chapter 2

# PERSONAL SOVEREIGNTY

To understand what it means to give yourself genuine authentic personal sovereignty is to understand your own innocence. This innocence means giving yourself absolute permission to accurately write the next chapters of your life exactly the way you want.

To actually have that kind of personal sovereignty is to understand your relationship with the process of creation itself. It is to give yourself permission to pen a most delightful future for yourself and for those who are walking this journey with you—the power of humanity personified. This is the space that holds miracles, having the personal sovereignty to validate *your* dreams as the most important potential of this moment. Truly, there are no limits, no boundaries. This human potential holds infinite possibilities. Just as a movie projector (or DVD player) can play any movie that is inserted into it, so too can your human consciousness embody any idea.

I like the idea of an old-school movie projector, the kind that was used in the big movie theaters. It had a really bright light bulb which created the light so that the image could shine or project onto the big screen. Then there was the movie itself which contained the story to be told.

This is a metaphor for our own life story playing out, a story that encompasses the specifics of what is happening in our own life. It is just like choosing a movie that you enjoy, and then watching it play out via a DVD player that streams the movie through your television set.

Going back to the example of the old-school movie projector, the light of the projector would cast light on the movie film, capturing the image, and then projecting it upon the screen, the place where the movie was actually experienced. This is just like the world around us, which provides the screen of our own movie on which we are living out our lives.

In this model of a projector, the bright light is our soul. It is the source of the movie, allowing it to happen at all. Because without the light of our soul, our lives would be over. Our "screen" would go dark, no movie. Without a soul, our body dies. The light of our soul embodies the light of infinite possibilities of any movie ever made. Our soul can play out any movie or story that we load into it, because it is our soul that is playing out this human role of an "actor" that is creating our human experience. It is your soul living as you now, *your* projector for this movie that we call life that you are living out right now.

The movie that is loaded in your projector is actually the energy of your own *karma*. It is the karmic signature of your own personal energy persona. This persona is the collective energy that is stored within your being. The unresolved mental and emotional patterning of your past is showing up in this present moment. Most of our storyline originates from the energy found within our own subconscious. To purify our energy is to shift the storyline. The script of our life is written in the energy of our own karmic disposition. In other words, the energy within our own personal energy persona creates the karmic tendencies of our own personal experiences.

Our soul can play out any story it wants, yet if we have unresolved karma within our own persona it is likely that the story that plays out will be more of the same, more of the past. The story we have loaded into our personal energy persona as our karma creates a momentum to our storyline, a tendency to experience more of the same, more of the past patterns repeating themselves over and over again. It is not until our karma is resolved that we can truly live the vision of our soul untethered.

The concept of every single citizen embodying this idea of being a king involves having dominion over one's own potential, absolute sovereignty over one's future, and permission to be director of the movie.

The collective achievement of being a king in our own kingdom has not come about in our culture en masse throughout the history of humanity, but it can happen now! For *you* are a powerful person. *Every* person embodies this human consciousness; every person is a point of presence of human consciousness. You are a point of *human* consciousness, and this human consciousness is the doorway to *all* possibilities.

What's new in today's world about the idea of being a king is that we now have the ability to tap into the potential of our human consciousness and bring it about into the kingdom with true personal freedom, personal sovereignty, and personal empowerment.

*Citizen King: The New Age of Power* represents a new age of power emanating from citizens acting like kings. Not citizens acting like kings with dominion over other citizens, but rather, citizens acting like kings in their own personal kingdom, in their own personal story, in their own personal potential. They create a flow of inspiration from the passion of their hearts, fulfilling the inspiration of their own dreams in an authentic and genuine way.

The soul's path is one of grace. To live an authentic life is to walk in grace on this earth. Just like a boat that creates ripples as it moves through the water, when you walk in step with your heart and soul, you leave behind you a wake of grace. It is in that state of grace that you feel *peace* within your heart every day. From that place of peace within your soul, you script the story of your life as you alone prefer. *Pure authentic you*, giving yourself permission to be the director of your own preferences, living the life that you choose.

I know this concept of being a king might not be in the forefront of your mind since we were not really raised to be kings. How common was the idea that you go to school, get an education, a job, click off 30 years working for the same company, and then retire? Where the core direction of your life was dictated by other people? Even the idea of having a single point of income was a very limiting factor.

What happens to that source of income lends itself to your own personal sense of security. Many of us have seen how volatile that idea can be. How can you be a king, with any sense of genuine personal sovereignty over your life, if so many of the fundamental aspects of how you live your life are attached to these volatile financial systems that have been so prevalent in our past?

The story of our collective past is one of deceit and betrayal. We have been removed from the director's chair. We have been corralled for containment in order to minimize the possibilities that we would most likely fulfill. We have been imprinted with a collective set of karmic impressions that mentally and emotionally detach us from our storyline and keep us in a state of mental and emotional reactions. We are not focused on our dreams, but rather, on the collective storyline that the media propagates, which prevents kings from discovering their own personal kingdom within themselves.

To truly be one that embodies the king within is to hone in on your most authentic preferences in each and every moment of every day. This is the place where self-love resides with exquisite permission to live the life of your dreams. For you to be able to embody such a storyline means you need to resolve and release the mental and emotional imprints of your past in order to understand how these karmic imprints have disconnected you from your own kingdom within.

For instance, to see an example of such karmic imprints, let us consider our currency. We share such a collective experience when we have a single monetary system on which we're all riding, and to which we are all attached. I mean, every single aspect of our lives is influenced by the idea of the value of the dollar, or any other currency. What happens to the value of that currency affects every aspect, every arena, of our own personal lives, and yet there are so many factors that influence the value of each currency. Our collective relationship with our currency is a core connection with our global monetary symbols and their perceived value, an agreed-upon value. The symbol of money is a collective agreement. This symbol of our particular country's currency is embedded in every major decision that we make.

We have assigned an agreed-upon role to this symbol. It shows up in deciding where we live, go to college, and take our vacations, what kind of car we drive, and whether we can afford health care. The current value of money, or currency, decides so many of the core decisions that we make in our lives. Since there are so many factors that decide the current value of the dollar, ruble, yen, peso, or any other currency, the value of our own money is always in a transition based on external factors, including a complete crash of established value.

It could easily be said that there are very many factors that influence the value of our lives, that in truth we are not actually free at all. There's no freedom in that. If the money you have in your savings account is shifting in value day by day because of external influences, how can you say you have any kind of a personal control or sovereignty over your life?

This isn't anything to be afraid of or to worry about, but rather, it's something to be conscious of so that we can move into a place where no one thing has such dominion over so many people on such a personal level. Since we weren't raised with the idea of having a genuine sense of control over our lives it can seem a bit daunting, a bit intimidating, to consider ourselves as kings. This is a context of our own personal life that we were never really encouraged to embrace. Yet every single one of us possesses this inner inspiration, this inner idea, of what our life can be.

Our soul has a dream of what is possible for our own life, of what a wonderful life would look like, the script to the story of our dreams coming true. It is a movie handcrafted and designed just for *you*. How many classes in school were taught about following our dreams? Detailed discussions about how to discern if an idea has come from our heart or our head? About how the ego is not needed to rationalize, approve or analyze the worthiness of our heart's desires. How the energetic signature of the dream *is* the dream itself as pure energy? How to capture a dream without diluting or polluting it, and then, step by step, bring it into creation? Very few, if any. Since our dreams are so important, so powerful for our lives, so powerful in a sense of our own personal fulfillment, then perhaps we should have been taught about our dreams in every single grade of school that we attended throughout our lives!

When individuals find their inspiration and value from within the very core of themselves, this disconnects them from being controlled or manipulated. If each individual—each citizen—understands their true power, then they have a genuine sense of personal sovereignty in their lives.

It is truly wonderful to discover that you have all the wisdom you need starting from the day you were born, and that it comes from your heart and soul. And *that* is a very powerful idea. Yet we weren't taught how to recognize this personal wisdom and use it in our lives. We weren't taught to truly own our lives in a very genuine way.

The old idea of a kingdom involved a single person playing the role of a king. Yet every one of us has an infinite well of inspiration present within us now. Every one of us is a soul playing out the role of BEing a human. Souls are very powerful. Every soul is an infinite well of inspiration. Your human age makes no difference regarding what your soul has to offer you; there are powerful ideas for every stage of your life.

The new idea of a kingdom is where everyone in the kingdom is honoring their own inner king, their own ocean of personal potential, living fully present in their own inspiration. Everyone feeling entitled to the free expression of their own inspiration. Everyone being connected to their own personal sense of what a wonderful life can feel like. A kingdom full of kings. A kingdom that actually honors all that we are capable of being. It affords each of us a full expression of our own potential. Not a single king per kingdom, but rather, a kingdom full of kings. That sounds much more divine and authentic to our human potential than the old, or former, king paradigm.

These ideas are very powerful. Because *you* are very powerful, both on an individual level and on a collective level. Don't be afraid to consider yourself a king. Don't be afraid to have total say in what happens in your life. The idea of the human experience comes from the process of creation that all of us are experiencing. The process of creation is always happening. Creation is a flow, *in*-spiration and *out* into effect. The process is starting from within us as an idea that we receive, as a moment of inner inspiration, which is then brought into creation through action.

# Chapter 3

# THE POWER OF CREATION

Creation is an inherent part of every single one of us. In fact, we are all creators in every moment of every day. To become conscious of that process, the process of creation, is to make ourselves powerful, very powerful, in an authentic sort of way. We can't escape the process of creation because it is in effect in every moment of every day. And when we become conscious of that process of creation, and then seed it with the inspiration of our heart and soul, then we have this authentic flow of creation where the vision, the dream of our own personal life, becomes the seed of this creative process.

When you become conscious of that flow and you allow the inspiration of your heart and soul to be the focus of your life, then your life expands as it should. The idea, that dream of your life, expands as it should. The dreams we have for our lives—the visions we have for our lives—are a reflection of who we are in the moment. As we honor the dream of our lives as fed to us by our heart and our soul we grow as individuals, giving us a genuine sense of satisfaction and fulfillment every day.

All of life seeks expansion, and you are that life itself. When you honor the inspiration of your heart and your soul, your life expands, and through that expansion you become a new person. That new person has new potential, and your heart and soul respond in kind with a new vision, a new dream of your life, that has expanded because *you* have expanded. There truly are no limits to this expansion; it is a process that cannot be exhausted.

When the inspiration—when the vision—of your life comes from within, there are no boundaries. There's no end-game. There's no day when it stops. It's an ever-evolving idea of what is possible for humans, both individually and collectively. When you apply that to the vision of your life, your future becomes truly wonder-full and full of excitement. The ever-evolving idea of life building upon itself, expanding upon itself, is a vision of our human potential. When each individual expands and grows, they bring new ideas and new resources to our human story, thus expanding the vision of our future individually and collectively.

When you start to ponder what possibilities the future could be holding for you, you start to expand your beliefs about what really could be created in your life. Once you start to genuinely trust that process you begin to get a glimpse of what Heaven on Earth could feel like. Individuals passionately creating the inspiration of their own heart and soul from within themselves. A sense of genuine trust of ourselves. Genuine trust of our hearts collectively walking in step with each other. It is a powerful place to live. It is an individual power and a collective power. It is the gateway to Heaven on Earth.

To be able to embody the idea of being a king at the personal level, with a newfound freedom and sovereignty, gives the individual *citizen* the opportunity to be truly powerful. The idea of *you* being *king* has not ever been entertained in our culture. The structure of humanity has always been based on a pyramid where there's a single point of control at the top that dictates what is possible for the kingdom. But this new idea of a Citizen King is different. The potential for it is finally achievable in the lives of the common man.

The reason that the new idea of being a king is so powerful is that no individuals have ever had true freedom on any large scale. If you observe the structure of our culture you'll see that there are so many aspects, so many ways, in which we have not achieved personal sovereignty in our lives.

The way our culture is set up today, there are many ways that our personal and individual lives are dictated by just a few core monopolies. If we look at our own personal lives, there are so many influences that dictate our access to the most fundamental resources of how we live our lives and what it takes to thrive. What I mean by that is that our culture has been built up based on the masses receiving their everyday resources from just a few sources. These core, fundamental industries are being controlled by just a few enormous corporations that wield influence over our personal lives.

For example, electricity. Electricity is essential to our lives. Electricity keeps us warm, and lights up our homes and communities.

Electricity provides power in such a fundamental way that, without electricity, we would have a very difficult time sustaining our lives. The current model of electricity is based on just a few power-generating plants for each city, single or few sources of electrical power per thousands of people. What happens to those few sources affects thousands of people. Renowned 20th century inventor Nikola Tesla, along with many others, have said that electricity exists in great abundance and can be provided to the masses for free.

Yet here we are, with single points of energy sources, set up so that you are required to pay to have a basic natural resource, single sources of electrical power that provide critical resources to millions of people in our cities. Whatever happens to those few sources of electrical power affects millions of people. If those few sources raise their prices, millions of people have no choice. There is no real sovereignty with electricity, even though it is found in great abundance in nature.

Electricity is just one example. Another example is fuel for your car. How many political systems influence the journey our fuel takes as it makes its way across the globe to be delivered to us? How reasonable is it that you can replace the source for your gas? Can *you* build a gas refinery by yourself, thus having personal sovereignty over how you get your fuel? Again, it is a kingdom of sorts, it is a monolithic structure, where the masses are dependent on very few sources of such a fundamental part of our lives.

How about the Internet? Credit cards? News and media sources? These core aspects of how we live our lives have been monopolized by corporations. There's been a tendency to take resources on many different levels and create monolithic systems. Where there is a "pay to play" mentality. If you want access to the news/media/movies, buy our services and we will deliver them to you. If you need gasoline for your car, buy that too, as it is part of the monolithic management of our everyday resources. What about your food? And your medicine? We'd love to manage that for you too. These are very profitable monolithic systems. During the recession of 2008, the oil industry made billions of dollars of profit, and was even subsidized by the taxpayers. There is no personal sovereignty there. How can you feel empowered to own your life when so many of the fundamental, needed resources are controlled by just a few?

I don't intend to focus on the problems of the past except to point out how they influence our own personal freedom, how these monolithic systems have diminished our own level of control in our everyday lives. To truly be a king is to have diverse choices in the fundamental resources of how we live our lives. Where nobody can interfere with you—with any of us—fulfilling our needs. That cannot be experienced unless we have the freedom of multiple choices in every fundamental arena of living. Where every critical aspect of our lives provides multiple choices for how we satisfy our fundamental needs. This will truly set us free. A genuine freedom that hasn't existed in our culture's past.

# Chapter 4

# CREATING CHOICES
# FOR HUMANITY

The new idea of personal freedom—freedom to be a king—comes from diversifying the fundamental resources of what it takes to sustain ourselves. For example, if your car breaks down you can open a web browser and find many, many pages of auto repair shops where you can go to get your car fixed. Well, to have so many choices gives you a sense of freedom. If one of those resources, one of those car repair shops, goes away, or doubles their prices, it doesn't change your life at all. There's another choice listed right below it.

It is through these choices that we have freedom. No choice—no power. No choice—no freedom. Multiple choices—much more power, much more freedom. So, if your electricity goes out, how many companies can you call to get your power restored? If the financial system goes out, how many different financial systems are there to fall back on? None, really. And this is a form of enslavement. This is a form of controlling the masses by controlling the choices.

In fact, humanity has been monopolized intentionally and deliberately for many centuries. But we are at the dawn of a new age where we are waking up collectively. We are waking up as a culture. We are waking up as a people. And we are starting to recognize how these fundamental resources have been structured in such a monolithic way, a monopoly over how the masses can sustain themselves. There is an immense amount of control in having the masses all dependent on a single system. Whoever owns, whoever controls, that single system has dominion, has sway, over the masses.

What happens if electricity doubles or triples in price, or fuel doubles or triples in price, or food, or any of the other fundamental aspects of how we live our lives? Who makes those choices? What events can influence those outcomes? How disconnected are you from that process? So how can you claim you have sovereignty over your own life if you don't have a say in the most fundamental aspects of living?

There's no power in having few choices. There's no power in having all of your resources monopolized by just a few corporations, a few power structures. How can you be a king in your own kingdom if the fundamental aspects of staying alive—if the fundamental aspects of living—are so decisively controlled by others?

So the new idea of being a king is to have a new kind of kingdom, a kingdom where the resources that sustain ourselves have been diversified and fulfilled by each citizen's inspiration. Where these core resources have been diversified by the citizens *themselves*, by following the inspiration of their own hearts. Where the citizens clearly recognize the power over the masses that these fundamental resources hold. Where the citizens recognize how these arenas of choices have been strictly limited. Where the citizen recognizes that bringing diversity to these core arenas is what is required to truly set all citizens free. Where the citizen recognizes the restrictions and limitations of choices when such core resources come from such few sources. *Citizen King* is about recognizing the fundamental structure of our culture and recognizing the limiting structures that have not served us in the past.

How can you be a king of your own kingdom if you have no choice in how life is lived out, if you have no choice in how the fundamental resources of your everyday life are dictated or fulfilled? When you start to think about it, the power of the individual is really quite limitless. Every single human being—human beings like you—hold within themselves so much potential and raw power. To bring that power about, and into effect citizen by citizen across the entire kingdom, brings a new idea of the future of humanity and the vision of what the kingdom can become.

Imagine if you had total freedom to create anything in the way you see fit, where you had multiple choices in how every single aspect of your life was fulfilled, and an authentic sense of sovereignty over the fundamental resources needed to live your life. Where instead of a monolithic-based structure where just a few control the choices of the masses, that pyramid was broken down into a honeycomb type of arrangement where it is divided into individual cells, and where there is not a single point of control over all of the cells. Where individual people recognize what genuine "power to the people" means. When we recognize that so many people have had so few choices in the past, we can now recognize that bringing new choices to the people is a very powerful concept to the individual as well as to the collective whole.

We are at the precipice of a shifting point in humanity that has so much potential—so much raw potential—that has yet to be fully tapped. The next revolution will be that of human consciousness, of human empowerment. To bring more choices to the masses holds immense potential for the entrepreneur who could provide those new channels of choices; it also provides an opportunity for commerce that hasn't existed before because humanity has been monopolized on so many different levels.

Each one of those monolithic systems provides an opportunity for an individual to create new choices for humanity. Your heart and your soul have ideas that can bring new choices to the masses. Those ideas are raw power. Those ideas that bring new choices to the masses hold raw potential for new commerce, new business, and new growth. We are talking about the involvement of millions, and even billions, of people on the planet.

When we recognize that bringing more choices to humanity offers an untapped bank of possibilities and potential that is really quite bottomless, we have the ability to create a whole new revolution. The industrial revolution was a mere drop in the bucket, so to speak, to humanity's evolvement because human consciousness—in both the individual and the collective —contains so much raw power.

Human consciousness is the most powerful substance on the planet. To bring more choices to human individuals all across the country, all across the planet, is to empower the most powerful substance on the planet in a new way. This draws a picture and an idea of a kingdom in the future that is really untethered.

Human consciousness untethered exemplifies an idea of a kingdom that is truly Heaven on Earth, where everyone is fulfilling the inspiration and passion of their soul. When the individual is set free by having the resources diversified and fulfilled by the passion of the heart and the soul of so many people, then commerce can be experienced at such an expanded level which the individual has never seen before.

This is the new kingdom. This is the new Heaven on Earth that awaits our desire to claim it. That awaits our desire to fulfill it. This next chapter of humanity is truly the most exciting time to be alive. The empowerment of human potential en masse. This idea transcends any border, country, ruler, or government. No institution, no government, no administration, is going to oversee this new kingdom because doing so would just recreate the monolithic structure that was previously in place.

The new platform for prosperity, for opulence in the kingdom, comes from within us—within you and from within me—basing our inspiration on our fulfillment from within and making the system immune from becoming captive again. True freedom comes from living within. The new kingdom is the kingdom within, the kingdom within you now. For each and every one of us is an unfolding story that has no end. Your potential to produce through passionate inspiration of your own self—of your own inspiration—cannot be depleted, ever.

There's always a new idea. There's always a new story. There's always a new chapter within each and every one of us. And when each of us as an individual has the freedom, has the personal sovereignty, to manifest our own inspiration without tether or restraint, then truly the Kingdom of Heaven—the Kingdom of Humanity—will thrive without end.

The ideas of inflation and recession will dissolve because those are based on monolithic structures. When we have a single monetary system, what happens to the idea of money—the symbol of money—ripples into every single aspect of our lives. When that monolithic structure is broken down and dissolved we won't collectively experience inflation and recession. Everything will ebb and flow by its own nature. It won't be a collective up and down. It will be free of those stories of the recession of 2008, and the depression of the 1930's, etc. This collective karma, so to speak, will never happen again. We will be free. As a whole, the structure of humanity has never been untethered. The potential of the individual has never been truly set free. So this next chapter of humanity is very exciting. This next chapter of humanity has so much potential. This next idea of what our kingdom can be is truly unlimited.

When humanity is allowed to express its passion and inspiration untethered, the imagination is challenged to be able to encompass the infinite possibilities. These are exciting times. We stand at the doorway of true prosperity in a way that has never been experienced en masse, perhaps ever before in the story of humanity on this planet. When you are finally able to have genuine sovereignty over your own personal kingdom, you have complete personal liberty. By writing your own personal story you have dominion over your own life. Untethered. Unlimited. Infinite possibilities expressed through you, as you.

The next chapter of our human story has the potential to be the greatest era of humanity. We are at that precipice, at that point, now. We are at that place of human consciousness now where we can recognize that potential. We can recognize what empowers the individual. We can recognize what would bring more choices to the masses. When we engage those ideas with the passion of our heart and soul, we will empower the immense potential of ourselves. There is so much potential present that it is truly a very exciting time to be alive. And here we are right now recognizing that. To take actions on that knowledge is to leverage our own potential toward shaping and sculpting our own future.

So are you ready to be a king? Are you ready to have a kingdom? Your own personal kingdom? That kingdom within yourself? Being a Citizen King means having dominion over your life. Citizen King means being able to leverage your own potential into effect. Citizen King is about showing up for your passion, your idea of what *heaven* would be for you. Do you deserve heaven? Do you deserve a kingdom? Do you deserve to be powerful?

These are ideas that have not been reinforced in our culture, educational system, media, or the storyline of what we've been told.

We haven't been taught to focus on our *personal power* in any kind of effective way, ever. Quite the contrary. Our society doesn't really grow legions of powerful people. However, when we recognize what gives an individual power and we build up a system with diversity and robustness, then the true power of our human potential can be fulfilled, untethered. How exciting is that? Raw human potential being fulfilled through a passionate expression of your heart and soul.

So don't be afraid to see yourself as a king. Don't be afraid of your own power. It can seem daunting at first, but that's only because we were never encouraged to embrace it. Your heart and your soul have a wisdom that transcends any condition in your life.

We're coming out of a very limited era of humanity. We have not been encouraged to genuinely embrace our power. We have not been encouraged to genuinely trust ourselves. We have not been encouraged to tap the infinite potential within ourselves. But when we take the steps to do these very things, we find a deep inner ocean of peace. We find a deep connection with life itself because we are that life itself personified.

You are here to be a creator of *your* human potential. When you honor that, your life expands. Your life is renewed. And this ripples into every arena of your life. When you honor the inspiration and allow it to come into creation—into fruition—in your life you become a new person, and life becomes fulfilling and satisfying. Life is renewed. Life becomes dynamic and alive. And that is a very rewarding place from which to live. It is, indeed, a very fulfilling place to live. When you learn how to live from that place you go to bed every night feeling fulfilled. You are literally a new person every day. Having fulfilled your passionate inspiration brings new chapters of your own life story into creation.

When we all embrace this idea of the creative process that is life itself as the core of who we are, it gives us permission to create. When we understand that the creative process is "on" 24 hours a day, seven days a week, it grants us an understanding that we were always intended to be the creators of our own lives. When we embrace the idea that our heart and our soul are an infinite well of inspiration seeking expression through ourselves, as ourselves, we can understand how life itself is intended to be a very fulfilling experience.

When we honor that by making choices and taking actions that expand our resources, where the individual—the citizen acting as a king—brings new choices to the screen that sets ourselves free, we are inviting and creating new possibilities for our future. It is only then that we can begin to move toward a genuine sense of authentic freedom where each person can live in personal sovereignty with the ability to follow their inspiration to fulfillment over and over again. That is where life expands, nurtures, and fulfills us individually and collectively. That is the seed of what Heaven on Earth looks like. And that is what now exists before us as true potential.

When we become cognizant of the idea that Heaven on Earth exists within our heart and soul now, and then embrace it with our thoughts, feelings and actions, we bring it into creation. We literally create Heaven on Earth, which is unconditional love personified. These are very powerful times. There are so many resources available to individual people. How much information can you get from the Internet in an hour? In a day? That was unheard of even twenty years ago. How many ways can your ideas be supported today compared to yesterday? Life is expanding at an incredible rate, and that is truly a powerful thing.

It is time for us to claim our power. Don't be afraid of it. It's an authentic part of you. It is more genuine than this "you" that your ego has created. Our *authentic self* cannot be diminished in any way. It is always there awaiting our desire for it. It is built in to the process of life itself. It is how life is hardwired. Life is a creative process expressed.

And you are that creation process now personified, just as you've always been. To become conscious of it and then to engage it in a conscious way brings a sense of knowingness, an understanding of what creation is all about. The process of creation is happening all the time. It is nothing to be afraid of. In fact, get excited about it, because it is genuinely exciting. Once you understand what your true potential is, if you don't get a big, authentic smile on your face, then perhaps you didn't truly understand it to begin with.

You are an eternal soul, a soul that has no understanding of fear. Your soul has no idea of the meaning of limitations. Your soul understands the value of what an ocean of infinite possibilities can provide to you, the human being, living out your life as the creator incarnate. So trust in your journey. Trust in *your* journey. You are here to fulfill your potential through the creative process that is ongoing in this moment and in every moment.

These are most exciting times. Allow yourself to get excited about *your* potential. About your future. About *our* potential collectively. And our future collectively. To be excited about what it would be like to live as a Citizen King.

So, are you ready? Are you ready to be a king? Are you ready to be a "power player"? Are you ready to show up for yourself and, thus, for humanity as well? I would like to suggest that if you are holding this book, if you are reading this story, if you are entertaining these ideas, that your heart and your soul *are* ready, and that you've taken the next step. So allow yourself to get excited about your life. Allow yourself to get excited about your possibilities. Excited about *your* potential. These next chapters of *Citizen King: The New Age of Power* are going to help you awaken to just that.

I invite you to step up and accept the role of being a king in your kingdom. Step up to your potential. Step up to the possibilities in your life and allow yourself to become the *king* of your own personal kingdom.

# Chapter 5

# OPENING THE DOOR TO YOUR DREAMS

You push the large, heavy wooden doors open and walk into the room. All eyes land on you. Your inspirations have brought you to this day. This moment. Today is the result of you following your inspiration. It was you honoring your potential that made your dreams come true. As you take your place you remember the journey that has brought you here, a journey that at one point in your life you never thought possible. Yet here you are. When the idea had first come to you it seemed improbable. Impossible. But you gave yourself the permission, the power, to hope.

As you look back over the journey you see the stepping stones, the incremental growth that changed who you are. That personal growth brought you into alignment with the very idea, the very dream you had, in that beginning moment. You trusted in yourself even through the darkness, even through those moments when the journey seemed difficult. The process, the power of creation, that has brought you here now is something you've learned to trust, to know.

A dream expands as you fulfill it. As one dream is fulfilled, another presents itself. You know that the idea, the dream, the inspiration that you have today will come about if you show up for it. Know that the vision your soul shows you is not only possible, but probable, if you simply trust the process itself and honor it with your thoughts and actions. To describe such a journey is to describe the creative process itself, the process of creation. It starts by learning how to trust the power of an idea. That idea comes into creation by moving yourself into alignment, into harmony, with the nature, vibration, and essence of what the idea represents. What the dream inspires. What the hope fulfills.

This journey I'm talking about has a million faces. You could be signing a contract that would open a new health center. Maybe you're launching your first screenplay, or publishing your first book. Perhaps you have finished designing your first product. Or maybe you just created a new surgical procedure that will save lives. What the journey is all about is incidental to the notion that you showed up for yourself. That you trusted yourself. That you completed the creative process yourself. When you first had the idea from your heart and soul, from the very essence of your being, the idea itself created an overwhelming sense of excitement, and here you are now fulfilling that dream. Once you have mastered the art of honoring an idea all the way through to completion, you have begun the process of genuinely mastering your personal power.

The process of creation is taking place in every moment of every day. To learn about and comprehend this process gives you an understanding of the steps to take. To practice and complete the process of conscious creation is to learn how to flex your *creation* muscle, how to fulfill your creative potential, and how to execute your personal power. Keep practicing this art of conscious creation until it becomes second nature to you.

This knowledge sets you free as the creator, as the king of creation, at this time, in this space. Your heart smiles now with the idea of what is possible for your life. That vision, that dream, of what your life can be. Your own personal kingdom is found within you now. In this moment, you are here now. This point of presence, this personal energy persona, this point of human consciousness that is you *now* holds the creative process itself. It is the process of all creation, for creation always starts with an idea, any idea, however big or small. It starts with a seed, and with an energetic signature that is the idea itself.

Energy, the native language of the universe, needs no human language or dialect to define itself. It has been engaged in fluent conversation and interactions from the beginning of time. The energy essence of the idea *is* the language to which the universe responds. We shape it with our words, thoughts and feelings. We boost it with our excitement and joy.

As a king you've learned to understand how powerful it is to free yourself from the bondage of posturing, the bondage of judgment, the bondage of stagnant beliefs, of emotional posturing. Like the canvas to a painter, to start with something fresh, something clean, is priceless. How can you bring a new creation about if there's already a tarnish on the canvas? How can you bring a new possibility—a miracle perhaps—into creation, if the canvas itself is tainted? If your own personal energy persona is diluted and polluted by the past, how can you create something pure? The purity of your own personal energy decides what kind of a range you have in the creative process. If you're holding on to large aspects of your past, then the majority of your own personal energy will perpetuate your experience of the past.

To *want* to be king of your own personal kingdom is the journey itself. There is no greed involved in it. It is the process of awakening itself. Consciousness is the creative substance of the universe. And you are that consciousness now. There is no end to your creative presence; the creation process is always on. It continually repeats itself. You cannot deplete the infinite field of possibilities by fulfilling your own inspiration. You don't deplete the potential of the universe by claiming and honoring your own inspiration. The creative process of the universe never ends. You can draw from it all you want, and it is always ready to create again.

By fulfilling every single dream you've ever had does not remove a single option, a single choice, a single possibility from your future. When you've learned to trust that, and know that, and own that as the creative presence that you are, then you can dream big and not flinch. You can experience life without any guilt or hesitation. To understand that you are always the creator is to claim your kingdom.

It is to claim your glory, the glory of knowing that it is God's good pleasure to give you the kingdom.

It is the universe's divine right to fulfill your expressions again and again, forever, because there is no other choice. The creation process is always on, whether you seed it with a new idea or not. The process of creation is going to happen either way. You are either consciously feeding it your intentions, or you have unconsciously let go of the rudder, and the universe will bring you more of your present experience of life. The creative process is always on. Whether you choose it consciously or you don't, the creative process will always take effect.

To claim your throne is to consciously claim your place in this creation process of the universe expressing itself here and now. Don't hesitate to claim your personal sovereignty in the authentic expression of your passions. The canvas of your creation is your own personal energy persona. It is the collective vibration of all of the energy encapsulated within your being now.

Claim your right to be king. Own it. Live it. Love it. Enjoy it. Fulfill it. That is the root of satisfaction. That is the root of fulfillment. That is the root of completion that brings a sense of peace to your being. Do you want peace in your own personal kingdom? Do you want peace in your heart? Then own your life. Claim your life. Live your life, as the king that you are now!

The kingdom is yours here and now, forever. It awaits your discovery of it. It awaits your excitement of it. It awaits your engagement of it. It awaits your joyful expression of it. Claim your entitlement to this creative process. Your own inspiration is the universe expressing itself as *you*. The infinite well of inspiration is within you now. You are forever entitled to fulfill your dreams as the creator incarnate that you are.

# Chapter 6

# GETTING CLEAR ABOUT YOUR DREAM

So what is *your* dream? Have you thought about it? Have you given it a clear definition? Is it in the forefront of your mind? Do you honor that notion, that idea, that vision, of what your kingdom can be? Of what your life can be? What are those images? What are those ideas that get you excited about your future? When you envision the future of your life, what ideas get you the most excited? What parts feel fulfilling to your own heart and soul?

Don't be afraid if they are big ideas. Don't be afraid if they are big visions. For you are here to express your *authentic self.* You are here to express the vision that your soul holds for your life. You are a point of presence of the creative impulse itself, an *individualized* point of presence of the creative process itself. You are experiencing the expression of your human potential. Flex that creative muscle. Fulfill your inspirations over and over again. Claim that creative potential by giving yourself permission to fulfill your inspirations with your attention and actions, until this becomes second nature as you master the art of creation itself.

Fulfilling your own inspiration starts by understanding the value of the *vision*. It starts by understanding the inspiration of the dream. It starts by understanding the joy and excitement of the process itself. It is the signature of your heart and your soul inspiring you to fulfillment. To freedom. To the joyful expression of your potential, of your possibilities.

Dare you dream big? Dare you dream bold? You're living on a planet where big and bold are not common characteristics of your fellow human beings. We were never taught to be truly powerful. We were never taught to be truly free. We were never taught to fulfill within ourselves our own personal sense of sovereignty as the infinite expression of consciousness, of creation itself.

Do you want to live in the most fantastic kingdom you can imagine? Do you deserve that? Can you claim that? Can you own that? Because the universe will gladly fulfill whatever you bring to the table. You can think big and you can think small, and either way it is fulfilled. For every expression is just a stepping stone in the infinite cycle of creation. No matter how big you dream and then fulfill those dreams, there is always another inspiration awaiting.

Dare to dream. Dare to hope. Dare to visualize a kingdom— your own personal kingdom—of what your life can be. And that is a seed. That is a point of inspiration put there by your soul to inspire you. Learn how to trust yourself, to show up for yourself. And the way you do that is to trust that your dreams, your ideas, are the very thing itself. The first step of fulfillment. The first step of satisfaction. The first step of personal expansion in a never-ending cycle of growth.

Your heart and your soul hold the story of an infinite journey for you that is without end. To honor the inspirations you are experiencing right now is to take the next step of an endless journey of creation. Flex your creative muscle. Flex the knowingness. Flex the understanding. Get intuitive about the creative process. Start with the vision that your heart and your soul are showing you now.

If I were to ask you, "What are your dreams for your future?" would you immediately start sharing them, speaking about them, because you already know them? Because you've spent the time visualizing, dreaming, and exploring the possibilities of what your life can be? Bringing them into your everyday consciousness?

Something as simple as writing them down brings them into physical form as an idea. To empower your dreams as a sense of genuine possibilities in your life is to take the time to fulfill them with your actions. And it also involves taking the time to actually sit down and write out the vision of what your future holds for you now.

The more time, the more attention that you bring to the idea—the vision of your dream—the more you are voting "yes" to your kingdom. The more you understand the process of creation, the more you claim your personal power. Do you deserve to be a king? Do you deserve to be powerful? Are *you* entitled to choose the big ideas? Are *you* entitled to fulfill your dreams? It is inherent to our very nature to do just that. Claim it. Live it. Own it. Your dreams are there for you to do just that. They will wait for eternity, or they can begin to be fulfilled now.

Which scenario do you choose? The kingdom that your soul has in mind for you awaits. That vision of your life is the purpose of life itself. To discover the truth of who you are. To fulfill your own potential, and then to do it again and again, living the life envisioned by your heart and soul.

When that day comes and you push the doors wide open, fulfilling your potential, it is in that moment that you have honored your purpose. What a feeling of joy and elation it is to celebrate the completion of the creative process. It is to live your dreams fulfilled, and to see your dreams played out on the movie screen of your life!

Dare you dream a wonderful dream? There is no end to the dreams and to the creations available to you in your kingdom. Your heart and your soul always have a new idea, a new vision, of another chapter of your life. There are no limits to what your kingdom can become. The universe isn't biased one way or the other. Choose the way that most fulfills *you*. For if you are not living in joy, if you are not feeling fulfilled, then the kingdom has been without a king, without *you* as its king.

# Chapter 7

# CAPTURING THE INSPIRATION OF YOUR HEART AND SOUL

The day is over. The sun is setting. A cool breeze blows through the bedroom window. It is time for rest. It is time for sleep. As you lay down on your inviting bed you totally let go of what your day looked like, and so you go to bed feeling totally fulfilled. You are feeling fulfilled on three levels: on a heart level, a soul level, and an ego level. When those three are fulfilled you experience satisfaction in all three arenas of your being. It's the trilogy of peaceful living. When you have flow equally in those arenas then every single day, at the end of the day, you go to bed feeling fulfilled.

Right now I am writing this sentence in this book, and so right now I am advancing this book toward publication. And by doing that, I will go to bed tonight feeling fulfilled that my heart and my soul's passion have moved closer toward fulfillment. I don't have to wait for the book to be published to have a sense of fulfillment from it. Just by honoring it *today*, it fulfills me. I don't ever worry about a day of salvation in the future, or the notion that I will be fulfilled *in the future*, or that I won't be living in happiness *until my dreams come true.*

Rather, I choose to be present to the inspiration of my soul *today*, in this moment. Taking actions on my inspirations *today* affords me happiness and joy in *every* day of my life. I can have happiness now, and enjoy life today. I don't have to wait until my journey is over, when really, all I am concerned about is that there was motion, *today,* and that an idea was turned into action at some level.

Your heart and your soul are feeding you with ideas. These ideas show up mixed in with your everyday thoughts. The key to recognizing the power of an idea is to understand from where it originated. Did the idea come from your heart and soul? Or did it come from your ego? On just how many of those ideas, generated from your heart and soul, do you take action? When you can answer that with a list of actions that you have fulfilled, then you know you have experienced flow. Taking action on our inspiration creates flow. That flow is very important, because without flow, you cannot get intuitive about the creative process. Why? Because it's not happening. You're not getting intuitive about how you go about creating because there are no actions bringing it into form. To bring an idea from inspiration into action is the flow of creation itself.

Many of us are very sensitive people, and we can start off intending to create flow, taking new actions on a new idea—a vision of our heart and soul. Perhaps you started writing a book, teaching new material in a class, or expressing your unique opinions about how things should be. Then perhaps you received critical feedback from someone, and since you're very sensitive, you immediately felt the impulse to shut down the creative process and stop the flow. You avoided taking more steps toward the completion of your inspiration because you got triggered by something you encountered, whether a person, a reply, or a judgment. And you began to feel upset.

This is not uncommon, whether you know it or not. The important part is simply to create flow. It can be as effortless as taking the simplest action to fulfill your inspiration. Do you want to be a king in your kingdom? Start taking action on your own inner inspiration. Start by capturing this inspiration by discerning when your thoughts are coming from your heart instead of your ego. Then you'll know that these are the ones you want to capture, that these are the ones to take note of and write down.

By writing down the inspirations of your heart and soul, you are capturing more information about what your dream looks like, about what actions will bring you the feeling of fulfillment at the end of the day. What would your actions look like when you are honoring your life purpose? Go buy some post-it notes (or some pads of paper) and put them by your evening nightstand, in the kitchen, and in the car with a pen close by. Later, when you are doing something else that is occupying your mind, out of the blue your heart and soul feed you a thought, a sentence or two: "Start teaching classes again." "Go for evening walks." "Read to the children at night." "Start writing your book."

It doesn't matter what the thought or sentence is about. The important part is that you don't rationalize it. Each sentence is approved immediately. No critical or analytical review by the *mind* or *ego* is needed. The minute the ink dries, it is available for you to take action on it. Don't think it over too much. Do make sure that you are taking care of your life. Do make sure you are always provided for. Sometimes the idea that you get from your heart and soul is so big that it will take you decades to accomplish. That doesn't mean you sell your house and move *today*, or quit your job *today*. It is always important that you take care of your life, and that any choice that you make that directly influences your life has been well-thought-out. But also understand that if an idea has presented itself from your heart and soul, that there *is* a way for it to come about. Don't let your ego vet your heart and your soul, for that could amount to karmic suicide. That is like letting the student (ego) correct the teacher (heart and soul).

To be clear, there is a time for everything. Be careful with your vitality. Don't quit your job, or move to another city, just because in one moment you have an overwhelming feeling that you were meant to be doing something else. Change can take longer than it seems. Be sure to always cover your bases. Make sure your choices and actions are always going to provide for the needs in your life, as well as the lives of those who depend on you. Don't quit your job until you *know* you will be provided for. Certainly, take notice of the big feelings, but also take the time to ensure that you are always provided for, that you will have the income and resources to keep your life viable and functioning well. Our expectations of how long something might take can be way off, especially if the idea is to start something completely new in our lives. Be careful and make sure your bases are covered all along the way.

When you receive inspiration that you know is from your heart or soul, know that there is, indeed, a way for it to be made manifest. Know that the idea is sound. Your soul can see a vision for your life that extends decades down the road. So stay connected with what works next. Trust in the ideas themselves. Don't let your ego edit any thought, or sentence, that your heart and your soul have given to you. Write them down, verbatim, on the post-it note, or on the pad of paper. When you receive ideas that further refine those thoughts, then write those ideas down too. And those refined ideas have now become action items for your ego. More importantly, you're letting your heart and your soul influence your everyday life. You're letting your heart and your soul take charge of the steering wheel of your life.

It's like you've been driving around in an old four-door sedan, and you're off in the desert knocking down cactus and bushes; it's as if there's a brick on the gas pedal. The car is filthy. It is layered with dust, dirt, and remnants of the paths you've crossed, because you are traveling cross-country. However, you are not actually driving on a road. You are not driving on pavement.

This is a metaphor for how difficult your life can become. Your mind and ego tend to try to manage the people and situations *outside* of you, attempting to create a sense of control and safety. When you start paying attention to what your heart and your soul have in mind for you by writing these thoughts down and then actually taking action on them, it is as if your soul reaches over your shoulder and grabs the steering wheel and starts pulling it left, because that's the direction in which the interstate is located. That's where the flippin' Autobahn is located. That's where living beyond your wildest dreams is going to be found. That is *you* fulfilling the vision of *your* heart and of *your* soul while your ego has the time of its life!

How does that sound? See, the cool part of it is that when you let your soul drive, your ego is let off the hook. Your ego has been roaming the desert while looking for the freeway, expecting to find people and situations outside of yourself that will bring a feeling of fulfillment. But lasting fulfillment is always an inside job. Your heart and soul not only know where the freeway is located, but it also knows where it will take you, making your dreams come true.

There are so many ways we miss the inspiration. We place our attention on our cell phones as we glance down at them. We put our attention on the news airing on TV, or via the Internet or radio, or on what has been posted to Facebook. And we place our attention on any number of other endless distractions, which are all external stimuli.

But what about your heart and soul? Place your attention there, so that you can catch the inspiration once it arrives. Then, when you write down that inspiration on a post-it note or other piece of paper, it becomes an action item for your ego. All that your ego has to do to make your heart and your soul have the fulfillment of accomplishing something today is to simply take action on the inspiration that has been captured in order to bring it about. That's all it takes. Accomplishing something. Anything. Nothing grand. Just something, *today*!

When you have accomplished that and you go to bed at night, your heart and soul will experience a sense of satisfaction. Your heart and soul will feel fulfilled. And you will genuinely feel complete, having honored *your* own purpose, and having honored *your* own passions. One happy king in one marvelous kingdom. Living from your own inner Heaven on Earth.

Your heart and soul feel fulfilled because your ego took action on what you wrote down on the post-it notes, those inspirations that came to you while you were doing something else, such as loading the laundry, unloading the groceries, getting out of the car, etc. It doesn't matter where the inspiration takes place; it only matters that you have captured it and then took action on it, because once you have taken action on the inspiration you have created flow.

The moment you start having more flow in your life, the more alive your intuition becomes. When there is no flow in your life you live from the perspective of your mind. The mind, or ego, compares choices with the past. The ego is motivated to make choices that are safe, because the outcome is known. But there's no flow in making choices based on the past. Flow comes from following new information; this new information is the inspiration itself. Without inspiration, there is no new information upon which to base your life. Flow by its very nature brings with it more information.

You start to become more intuitive when you begin paying closer attention to your heart and your soul. Just like flexing a muscle, the more you do it, the more responsive it becomes. When you start to become intuitive and start acting from that place of intuition, the *more* of your choices move closer into alignment with the vision of your heart and soul, and the more you begin to experience a sense of synchronicity in your life.

The more you can live in that space of listening to your heart and soul, the more peace you will feel within yourself, and the more your choices move into alignment with your dreams coming true. The more time you spend thinking about what you prefer, the easier it is to make choices that are in alignment with what you prefer.

When you get authentic about what you genuinely prefer and you own your life enough that no one can sway you from that, then you become a fulfilled person. Everything about you becomes more passionate, electric, alive, and fulfilling. When you can live in that space over and over again you are literally making your dreams come true. Heaven on Earth. King in the kingdom. You're rockin' this place because you own this place, not in a commanding or controlling sort of way, but in a genuinely "let's do it" sort of way—in a "let's have fun" kind of way. Do it any way you choose—just do it.

A good way to tell if you are following your heart and soul is if your ego feels excitement and joy, and if you move through your day enJOYing what you are doing. What did you enjoy about today? What are you enjoying about now? When you start paying attention to what you enjoy, you know which choices your ego can make to be in alignment with your heart and soul, for the vision of your life is always compatible with your happiness. When your ego understands where your heart and soul intend to take your life, you feel genuinely excited about how your life is going to play out. To honor the vision of your heart and soul brings a sense of awe and amazement about what your life can actually be.

When you can get your ego to enjoy life, and when your heart and soul are feeling fulfilled because you are completing the inspiration captured on the post-it notes, then you are genuinely taking on the role of being a king in your own kingdom. Then the passion and vision of your soul become a legacy fulfilled, a powerful contribution, to this chapter of humanity that is unfolding on this planet Earth *now*. You are that important. You are that powerful. You are here to become a king.

What will it be that you choose? Will it be purity of heart? To get good at making your heart and soul feel fulfilled is to purify your heart. That purity is created through forgiveness and compassion. When you are able to forgive everyone in your life including yourself, and when you have compassion for everyone in your life including yourself without condition, then your wand starts to work. Then the storyline of your life becomes expanded, limitless, and exciting. Then you can envision any movie that you want to create in your life, and the universe will mirror it back to you. Ask, and it is given!

Your heart and soul write the screenplay of your life. They are the authors of the script of *your* movie. You are the creator, co-creating with the universe. You are the director of the movie of your own life. That's how powerful you are.

# Chapter 8

# LIVING FROM YOUR HEART

When we step into our authentic story, and engage the flow by taking actions, we create an outcome. And whether we are a powerful person or not, playing out our authentic story has to do with the purity level of our heart. Why is purity of heart important? Well, it's not required by any means. There are plenty of hearts out there that aren't very pure. But that's part of the karmic signature of this beautiful planet on which we are living now.

Purity of heart is important as a choice if you intend to be a powerful person. Purity of your heart decides how much of humanity you are able to love unconditionally in every moment. When your heart is pure and you can look at any face of humanity—the hero and the villain, the saint and the sinner, the cop and the criminal—and when you can look at any personification of the human experience and say, "But of course!", the universe has no bias against our freedom in making any choice we want. We are making these choices motivated by our own karma, without the ability to err, for it has taken us many lifetimes to accumulate such deep layers of darkness. Yet our souls chose this darkness as an advanced karmic classroom, of sorts, in order to gain an opportunity to learn the most powerful lessons possible for mastering our human nature. If you can discover your light when the world around you is playing out such darkness, then that itself is the most advanced lesson you can have in the karmic nature of our human demeanor. Yet there is nothing to worry about—no karmic law has ever been broken. No human on the planet has ever violated a karmic law. We are all innocent.

We are actually an ocean of souls who have incarnated to play out this time in our human history. And what a time it is. There is so much human desire for change right now. That itself is raw power, a huge idea that has not fully manifested yet. And here you are, walking among the humans playing out this story. You have a life history that describes your life, and your karma has had a lot of influence on how you experienced that.

Our karma is like a running history of what we have not yet resolved from our past, an energetic history of what we have not accepted about the nature of being human. No karma can be accumulated if every single thing that is happening in the moment, in the *now*, is unconditionally accepted—as if you chose it that way to begin with.

Another way to look at it is as if we are living out this huge play, with billions of actors playing out their own individual roles. Behind every part for the actors in this play, there is a soul. Each soul has chosen a karmic lesson to be learned. Each human has a karmic propensity with a lesson attached to it. The karmic laws themselves are impersonal. Karma is indifferent to your choices, with no bias of its own. In any moment, we can choose to accumulate karma, or release karma. It is only through our human nature that karma can be experienced as either suffering or joy. Karma itself has no pain or pleasure associated with it; it is only our judgment of our experience of it that produces one or the other.

The story you decide to play out in your life is created by the ego until you learn how to follow your heart. Then the story becomes the dream your soul had in mind for you before you were even born. Once you hone in on what that dream looks like, your heart takes over driving your life in the direction it most wants to go. And the action, or flow, is created when *you* actually take action on the inspiration of your heart and soul. So dial into that vision of *you* living the most opulent life possible. Honor your authentic preferences, and *you* will have the time of *your* life.

To be able to genuinely honor your dream is to live a life of joy, to allow the flow, and let go of how big the dream gets. Just show up in each moment, and follow your heart. Get that down to a reflex, and all of the boundaries dissolve, with complete and total trust of *your* own heart. Establish an ongoing dialogue with your heart, in order to know when your heart is guiding you. Place value on that inspiration and learn how to trust it, then follow it without hesitation or justification, with total freedom to be authentically *you*.

By understanding that every soul has exquisite permission to play out its role, you realize that *your* role is always approved without the need for anyone's permission. So trust in your part of this human story. Any role, no matter how horrible it may appear to others, is within the realm of the karmic lessons that we are here to learn. Under it all, we are all the same, a soul playing out our part. From that perspective, forgiveness affords a shift in the script, a new scene written in the story. The mirror of the universe has no bias of its own. It is the soul that can conjure up the vision, and then actually bring it about, that will create Heaven on Earth.

We have stood by and watched so many horrendous chapters of human suffering unfold. But our past has no power of its own, only what we believe of it. We are entering a new doorway to the future, one that can be seeded with an idea. Now we can understand how the dreams of our hearts can actually come into creation, cleaning out your karmic energy persona with compassion and forgiveness. By giving yourself permission to forgive every aspect of your past, every scene that you have ever played out, you in turn can forgive every action carried out by every actor in this collective storyline of our humanity.

When you can forgive and move into compassion for every single life story that is playing out, you are entering the arena of unconditional love and acceptance for the many faces of humanity. The lessons we came here to learn, even the more sinister lessons of war, struggle and suffering, have given us the opportunity to learn the more advanced karmic lessons. When you understand that the projector, the DVD player, has no bias as to what story it is playing, and that every storyline playing out now is a reflection of our collective karma personified as an individual like you and me, then you understand that just as you cannot create any fault karmically, neither can anybody else. And so you're off the hook, and so is everyone else. We are all innocent.

You are playing out this human story from the vantage point of your soul, your soul before you personified as a human. And you'll still be a soul after you leave this earth. Your soul is the most authentic part of you. When your soul chose this lifetime it included karmic lessons threaded into the storyline that were perfect for what you came here to learn karmically. When you trust that your journey was handpicked, as were all the others, there's this sense of elegance, a sense of grace, that you experience. You're off the hook. You're free to choose as you desire. The universe will never say "no." It only knows "yes."

To purify your heart is to purify yourself. To be able to love from your heart is to be able to love yourself. You cannot love another individual outside of the scope of the love you have for yourself. To learn how to love yourself is to metaphorically clean the lens of love that allows clarity and flow between yourself and the collective human condition. When you can hold the space of love for the story that is playing out now, it is through your presence that love can change the storyline, creating a new opportunity for a new outcome.

Your heart is like a high-power amplifier broadcasting the inspiration of your soul. The more pure your heart, the more vivid is the energetic image that you can project from your persona, which the universe will in turn mirror back to you. As you cleanse your heart, you open up new paradigms of what is possible for your life, of what is possible for you to become.

It's like going into a DVD store that doesn't offer many choices, just a few movie genres, very few choices. You're feeling karmically laden. You're loaded up. And you're playing out the familiar storyline of what your life has been, this karmic story that has been recorded in your subconscious as a history of all the different moments in which you couldn't accept what was happening in the moment. And now here you are carrying around this karmic baggage, with each energetic component of your karma being a reflection of some aspect of our human condition in which your soul wanted to gain more experience—and here you are playing it out.

To be able to change the story is to be able to accept the divinity of the story, just the way it is. That acceptance affords you the ability to stay in your preferences, thus creating the energetic vote for your future. Acceptance allows you to stay in the vibration of your heart and soul. Had you re-acted to the story, your energy would have shifted, and thus your energetic vote for the moment would have been lost in the re-action. Every re-action creates the same re-sults.

The possibilities for change increase as you are more able to stay in the vibration of your own inspiration. Keeping guard over that authentic vibration allows authentic flow into your life. When you allow authentic flow, you allow the story to change. If there's no authentic flow, the story is not changing. Re-actions interrupt authentic flow. To catch yourself re-acting is to catch yourself perpetuating your karma. It is your feelings, thoughts and beliefs that trigger your re-actions.

If you find yourself re-acting to the external story by being judgmental or projecting your beliefs, then you are shifting the energy of *you* based on the stories of the external mindset. You have fallen out of alignment with *your* innermost self. To witness the difficulties of the past externally in the media and online, and yet accept them as just another form of creation as chosen by other souls just like you, affords you the ability to stay in your *authentic* vibration, thus voting for the dream within you and not more of the past storyline.

Staying in that authentic space keeps the creative process seeded with the vision of *your* dream. Re-actions to other people's choices stop flow. If there's no flow in you, then you are not a king playing the creator in the kingdom. If there is no flow, there is no new creation happening. It's as if you've pressed pause on the movie so that you can repeat the karmic signature of what your subconscious and conscious mind are projecting to the universe at this moment. The storyline karmically becomes static and repetitive.

The more you purify your heart, the more volume you can create in your flow, which is an increased volume of energy that is, indeed, your human consciousness. When you purify your heart you are cleaning the karmic lens, and bringing new resolution to the image of the energy broadcasting out of you now. Your personal energy persona always includes this collective emanation of your subconscious and conscious energy that the universe turns around and reflects back to you as people, situations, and circumstances that play out the karmic storyline of *your* life.

When you open up to flow and become intuitive with *your* story, *your* adventure, *your* lessons, and you come to peace with them, then you are experiencing the perfect storyline in which to master each element of your karmic collage. Because when we are living in a place of peace, we can recognize when we drop into re-action. It is only from that place of peace that we can clearly see the broader scope of our karmic propensities. To live in peace is to live in power.

When you feel the energy of your karma arise from your subconscious you'll note that it is a familiar feeling. It doesn't matter if it feels good or bad. It feels familiar. Good or bad, it is something you have experienced, and the karmic lesson is to understand why it is there, as well as the story that it has to tell you. This then affords you the ability to release it in the moment based on the purity level of your heart. Your heart is the passageway, the gateway, to forgiveness and compassion.

Forgiveness and compassion are the heavy-duty cleaning tools of our karmic energy persona. The more you purify your heart, the more you love yourself and humanity unconditionally. The more decisive your control of the storyline becomes, the more it affords your heart and soul the ability to project your dreams; then the universe has no choice but to reflect that back to you. Your heart and your soul now become the only energy in your personal energy persona, your energetic signature of the moment.

And that's soul-level living. That's your soul untethered. That's *pure authentic you!* That's *new humans* living on the planet as unconditional love. Kings living in their own kingdom. Soul-level dreaming. Soul-level visioning. Soul-level utopia. You become a never-ending wave of passion and creativity expressing itself in the moment as your ego continues making choices that keep it—keep you—in joy all day. A king living as one in his or her own kingdom. *Pure authentic you.*

To be a king is to understand the power of pure energy. To be a king is to understand how to capture the inspiration of a vision energetically, without polluting or diluting it. To be a king is to focus on your inspiration with unconditional love, setting up your ability to leverage your highest possible power and be fully present in that moment, in that *now*. To be a king is to direct the storyline of your future that is unfolding in each and every moment.

You are a new *Citizen King* fulfilling your dreams.

# Chapter 9

# LIVING IN THE KINGDOM OF THE HEART

For each of us to be a king genuinely and authentically, a king empowered, is to experience self-love. The love of self. The forgiveness of self. The compassion for self. The idea is that you are at peace with everything that has happened in your past to the point where you have achieved absolute acceptance, where you have reached a place of total acceptance of all aspects of your life story. You have come to a place of absolute transparency with your own past so that you can look at every story, every paradigm, that has played out in your life and say, "But of course!"

Because in truth, the universe isn't biased at all; it shows up innocent in every moment. There is no posturing. There is no underlying preference from the universe. It will gladly manifest your desires. It will gladly mirror any idea or any dream that it is fed. A mirror doesn't choose which images it will reflect and which ones it won't. It is unbiased toward all images. Just like a projector at a theater, it is unbiased about what film you put in it and play. Just as a DVD player is unbiased about what DVD you play, you can live any story you want and the universe will gladly mirror it back.

To understand that, and then give yourself permission to show up in your life and become consciously aware of what you're energetically emitting to the mirror—the image, the energetic image of your persona—is to live in pure authentic alignment with your heart and your soul's dream. And when there's no other energy contrary to that, then you have released and healed your past. In that moment, in that space, in that clarity, you have fulfilled the idea of your soul through a process of never-ending creation, bringing ideas into feelings, into effect, over and over again.

You have flow, and you are intuitive about that flow. You trust the flow of this endless stream of inspiration from your heart and soul. You are vividly conscious of the idea that your human body does not dictate your life. You are a soul before you took on a human body. When the human body is gone you are still a soul.

You are timeless, regardless of what storyline plays out here on the planet. You are a timeless soul experiencing what it means to be the species of human being on a planet called Earth. You can look at other species and see a demeanor that is inherent within that species. For instance, you can understand the innocence of a bunny rabbit, the aggressiveness of a lion, and the gentle nature of a butterfly, and also understand that the human being species has certain tendencies as well. To understand the nature of these human tendencies and how you are personally playing them out on your own, is to give yourself permission to be a genuine and authentic human being.

Imagine for a moment that you are walking out in the forest and you come across a deer. The deer has no need or desire to be a tree, or a flower, or a human. It is completely at ease with being a deer. A flower doesn't long to be a dolphin, or a mountain, or a bird. So too will you be totally accepting of the fact that you are a human being.

You have this human being persona and it has a lineage, a life history, loaded with these karmic lessons of varying degrees of density or darkness. You know that every single life story that you have ever played out has never, ever, broken a karmic law. Period. You are innocent now. Period. You are innocent forever. Period. To give yourself absolute clarity in that truth affords you the permission slip, affords you the permission, to show up as a genuine and authentic king of your kingdom. It is God's good pleasure to give you the kingdom. It is the mirror's good pleasure to reflect back to you the vibration of your own energy.

When you can truly understand that you are here just to be a human being, then you can relax and be yourself, fulfilling the vision of your soul. When you can take action on that vision every day, just know that simple steps will suffice. Any flow at all moves you closer to your dreams. When you are writing down your ideas, you are writing down the inspiration that your heart and soul are feeding you, and you are taking action on it. As long as you are taking action, you have flow. As long as you have flow, you have the ability to change your karmic signature. As long as you have the ability to change your karmic signature, you can choose those choices that move you more into alignment with the authentic vibration of the idea, or dream, that your heart and your soul are holding for your life now.

When you can consciously make choices that move you into energetic alignment with that vision of your heart and your soul, you are fulfilling the Citizen King archetype. You are moving into more of an alignment with yourself. The inherent byproducts of this are a sense of peace, a sense of genuine peace, an ocean of peace that swells from within your being.

At the end of the day when you can attain peace with this human BEing experience that you are living out today and tomorrow, and when you are at peace with your role of living as a human being on this planet, just know that your role of simply being a human is perfect and divinely ordained. And know, then, that it is the exact expression of who you are supposed to be.

When you know that your life path is a Divine expression, a Divine movie, a Divine idea, *you* personified, that is when you can genuinely have compassion and forgiveness for yourself, because to show up as a powerful king you have to have an absolute sense of permission; you cannot have an absolute sense of permission unless you have an absolute sense of innocence. If you hold guilt in relationship with the choices of your past, you hold the idea that any of your choices can be guilty of "sin," and this idea of "sin" is a man-made idea.

To give yourself permission to be the writer, director and actor of your own *heart and soul movie*, affords you the ability to write the script to keep you in alignment with what you prefer. Your soul is the producer. It will figure out the how, and feed it to you as your own inspiration. It knows what would bring you the most joy. Get out of your own way and let your soul drive. You are entitled to everything that is relevant to you. The mirror merely reflects it back to you. The projector or DVD player can tell any story; you as the writer can create any story or idea, and then start refining it and fulfilling it.

In order for you to be king means to genuinely be able to bring into creation any inspiration that springs forth from your heart and soul. You have given yourself permission to value your dreams. You have given yourself permission to empower the validity of your dreams as a Divine expression of the infinite choices of what is possible in our human form.

When you can embody that with a sense of peace, empowerment, and entitlement—an absolute sense of permission—then you will genuinely be a king in a kingdom. Your kingdom. Your vision. Your dream. And your dream will come true. Your ego will do hand-springs down the street, and your heart will jump for joy as you fulfill the Divine idea of what your life can be.

# Chapter 10

# GRANTING YOURSELF
# PERMISSION TO BE KING

It is important to understand your innocence. You are a human being playing out a life story. Your life is the projector on which the vision of your soul is playing out. Just like a DVD player does not care what movie is playing, the universe will gladly reflect back to you every energetic story it receives. So how pure are you able to energetically cleanse yourself? To cleanse the karmic energy in your subconscious is to release the influence of your past. The energy in your subconscious provides the karmic momentum to your life story. You cannot really change the direction of your life if the majority of the karma in your subconscious has not been resolved.

To truly walk as a king is to know your truth. It is to embody your authentic self. There are three core energetic entities in this karmic equation, your mind (thoughts and beliefs), your feelings (emotions), and your heart/soul. When you have a lot of karma playing out in your life, you are experiencing mostly mental and emotional energies caught in a pattern, or wave, of re-action. When we find ourselves re-acting to our karmic triggers we cannot genuinely follow the inspiration of our heart and soul. When we haven't resolved our karma, we tend to be sensitive to our environment, where the re-actions of others trigger our own re-actions. That is when we lose our power. It is not until we have resolved the karma in our subconscious that we can truly know our power. Yet the presence of our karma cannot ever erase the kingdom within us; the kingdom always awaits our return to it. Our soul always holds the vision of our kingdom for us to claim. When we can load the DVD player with the vision of our soul we will be a king living in our own personal kingdom.

The land of kings embodies a place where everyone follows their own inner passions and their own inner dreams of what their lives can be. There is no violence, war, struggling or suffering. When you go within, there resides a kingdom of peace. Resolve your emotional/mental posturing, and shift your consciousness over to the stream of inspiration that is pouring into you in this and every moment. When you quiet your mind, you can then find an ocean of peace, knowing the DVD player is playing out your movie with nary a fret. Perfect. You are free to dream up your dream. The DVD player always says "yes." Carte blanche (in other words, you can have whatever you want based on your preferences). You are a powerful person. We all are. An infinite well of potential. So go ahead and dream *big*. You deserve it.

In order for you to genuinely feel like a king in your own kingdom, you have to feel like you have permission to make any choice that you choose. I mean, a king is the ultimate decision-maker, the ultimate form of governance. The idea of a *Citizen King* is *you* as a citizen living with the wisdom of the king in your own kingdom, the kingdom within you now.

In order for you to show up as a king is to give yourself permission to make any choice that resonates with your heart and soul. You can make any choice that resonates with your ego, but the ego tends to be vested in the conditions that are outside of us. The ego tends to have a preference, a posture, with the various elements within our own lives, and as such, when the ego becomes creative, it tends to be a projection of those karmic patterns in which it is vested.

In order to move from the perspective of being a citizen, to becoming a *Citizen King*, is to step out of those prior patterns that your ego has encountered during your entire life. It is to step out of those patterns and be free enough with your imagination that you can capture the idea of what your personal kingdom could look like.

Maybe it's a 40-acre horse ranch in the country. Maybe it's starting a speakers bureau. Maybe it's writing a screenplay. Oftentimes the ideas, the inspiration, that our hearts and souls feed us for how we can live our lives exist so far outside of the patterned addictions of the ego.

When those ideas that emanate from our heart and soul are so profound, so visionary for our own life, often the very next thought we have involves rationalization, because our awareness has moved back up into our head, and out of our heart. "Well, I can't do that, 40 acres ... I mean, I'm still living in an apartment." And so the ego tends to quantify and contextualize ideas based on the past. It is very difficult to be a king if the ego is the one making the choices.

The idea of being a king is to purify your heart, the power amplifier of your persona. To genuinely trust in the vision of your heart is to say yes to your dreams. "Well yes, yes, a 40-acre ranch! In fact, I was thinking something more like 45 acres, and not only a horse ranch, but also raising llamas too. I would *love* that!" When the ego gets excited about the vision because it actually trusts that there is a way for it to come about, then joy fills your being. You start to feel excited about your life path more and more every day.

Often, we were taught values based on being a citizen, how citizens behaved, and where they belonged in a society. With those values it would be difficult to play out the powerful visions of what it would mean to be a king. To truly be able to embody the power, the role that a king plays out, is to understand the value of the dream, what Heaven on Earth would actually feel like. When a king engages the choices before him, he needs to recognize the value that the vision has to offer, in order to place the value of the vision above the old story of the past, thus empowering the fulfillment of the vision.

Our parents were raised to be citizens, a byproduct of their upbringing. Often, we were taught that our individual role was merely to be a citizen, and that the direction of the kingdom was decided by others. We have never collectively been taught how to be powerful. Our culture raised us to be citizens. It taught us what our roles were to be in life, as well as how we should value our life. Those imprinted values decided at what scope, or scale, we could embody a new idea for our own life. How could we embody the vision of a king if we saw ourselves only as citizens? Oftentimes, as citizens, we can feel intimidated by the grandeur of the vision of our soul, as if it is beyond what we think we are capable of being to influence society in such a powerful way.

We can feel out of place when we see how our soul intends us to influence humanity. Who are you to have an idea that changes the course of history? Who are you to be the inspired one that brings a whole new outcome to our human condition? Can you be one of the citizens, acting as a king, who changes our collective story? Is that role appropriate for you? There will be others who will change the course of humanity, and that possibility to effect change on a large scale exists for all of us. To be king is to genuinely trust the vision of your soul as the perfect idea of your life story. These times are calling us to claim our power. Humanity is looking for powerful people to bring a sense of balance back to our human condition, to bring a vision of what is possible for humanity to experience, and a genuine sense of peace and prosperity for all mankind. Can you dream that big? Can you dream that bold? Who are you to be the game-changer? If not you, then who?

There are arenas of choices that you already feel empowered to make, yet the choices that your soul has in mind for you tend to stretch your sense of personal power. To be able to make powerful choices is to be able to create a new sense of empowerment. It's like you've been living out the movie of your life as a citizen, which has been playing on a single DVD. Then suddenly you recognize that you can press pause, eject, and remove the DVD at any time. You can even go to the DVD super-megastore and exchange the DVD of the life you have been living for a different DVD, a DVD of any genre of your choosing, any genre that you are able to embody energetically.

And that is the key to being a king in your kingdom. To be able to embody the exact vibration of your inspiration is to bring it into reality, and present it to the universe as the mirror that it is, without flaw or distortion.

Think back to when you were 13, 14, or maybe 15 years old. You're living in the midst of your family dynamics, and there's a knock on the door, "Clunk, clunk, clunk." You look up at your dad, or mom—whoever made the critical choices in the family—and they stop what they're doing and look at the door. As they walk over to answer the door you sit there and watch. The door opens and there's a person standing outside the door. You can't see who it is. And it speaks to your father or your mother.

After the conversation is over, the door closes. And then you hear a story about how your family is going to pick up and move to another city, or perhaps to another state, or even country. Or maybe it's a story about how mom can go back to college now. Or a story that dad is going to start a better-paying job.

So in that situation, think of who could have possibly been knocking on the door to persuade your family to make a life-critical choice. Was it a representative from a particular religion? Was it the pastor, priest or pontiff from a church? Was it a government official? Was it a boss? A current employer? A new employer? A school administrator? A relative? Who could that person have been? Think back to your family dynamics and look at where power was authorized, where power was permitted.

Think back to what aspects of your culture could dictate your choices for you. This can help you understand which aspects of society had dominion over your household, and who could have had such a decisive influence over your family's choices, as well as which part of the culture's values had dominion over fundamental family choices.

In my family it was certainly religion. It was the church knocking at the door. And it would have been my dad answering the door. Whatever in the world the church could have possibly asked of us, we certainly would have done, verbatim. No questions asked. It is that exquisite permission, the idea that "it has been spoken and now it shall be," that we want our heart and soul to have in our lives in order for us to genuinely be a king.

Why is this important? If you can't have that kind of absolute say in your own life, then you are actually living someone else's values and expectations. To give your own heart and soul that kind of absolute permission to guide you as the ultimate say in what happens in your life, is to truly be free. Because if you are not feeling fulfilled at your heart and soul level, you are not genuinely feeling triumphant in your own kingdom. You do not actually enjoy a sense of personal sovereignty. You do not give yourself unconditional permission to completely decide your life choices as you prefer. You're not genuinely embodying the idea of you being a king.

Countless people on the planet aren't seeing themselves in a very respectful light. But when you can do so—when you can give your heart and soul carte blanche to create an idea of your life, and then do so to the point that when the inspiration arrives not one single vetting process is required of the ego—then the idea is already approved. Done. Just like that.

When you can reach that kind of approval rate, and then speed up the sequencing of the inspiration to the point that you can be inspired multiple times in a single month, or even week, or day, then the inspiration of your heart and your soul is being fulfilled by taking that inspiration into action by your ego. It is becoming fulfilled in a never-ending stream of inspiration.

And what is the beauty of this? Well, you can feel like a king, and you can actually be a king, *today!* You can feel like a king right now. It is not that your dream has to come to fruition now. It is that you have taken the steps to start fulfilling the dream. That's it. Period. Because the dream is ever-unfolding. Your dreams are a stepping-stone of what is possible in your life. And the only thing that dictates whether you're moving toward them or not is flow, and that flow takes place when your ego takes action on the inspiration it receives from your heart and your soul.

When you receive inspiration from your heart and soul, the inspiration becomes an action-item for your ego. Your ego is off the hook as far as trying to manipulate the environment outside of you; rather, it becomes fulfilled by taking steps, by taking actions, however simple they are, *today*. When you move your choices to the inspiration that is coming from within you, you empower your heart and soul as the creators of your life.

When you can take an action toward your dreams coming true every day, every week, every month, and every hour, then your heart, your soul, and your mind are fulfilled in that day, in that moment. And you are living a fulfilled life. You feel that you have honored your potential. You feel that you have governed the idea of your life in a promotional and an expansive way, allowing flow into your life. And when that flow is part of your everyday life, then your life is rich, full, and rewarding. That is *you* living as a king in your kingdom. That is *you* fulfilling your potential. That is *pure authentic you* feeling validated, worthy, entitled, and honoring the inspiration of your heart and soul.

When living an inspired life becomes part of your natural, everyday existence, then you're living in Heaven on Earth. Your Heaven on Earth. A king in your kingdom. There's a sense of glory to that. There's a sense of grace. There's a sense of eloquence. Life knows what to do. Your heart and your soul know what to do. You don't have to fret about whether or not you're doing the right thing. You can never do it wrong. You can never get it all done. The DVD player will gladly play another tale. It's just a matter of what you are feeding it as an idea, a story, a script, and how that story is in alignment with your potential and your passion.

Is the story that you are playing out now in your life fulfilling your purpose? Because when those aspects of your life are fulfilled, then all of you—your heart, soul, and mind—are living the dream. Living *your* dream. Rockin' life. Living life large. Untethered. Wide open. So dare you embody your dreams? Dare you value your dreams? Dare you honor your dreams with the actions that will fulfill them? Master the art of expanding the flow in your life, and your dreams *will* come true.

# Chapter 11

# BECOMING PURE

To be a king is to own your kingdom in the sense of what you are experiencing. It is to own it in the sense of understanding the nature of the creative process, how indifferent it is, and then getting into that authentic, genuine alignment with that *you*. And living in that pure, authentic space that is found in your heart and soul. That space is purity. And the reason we're talking about purity is because the purity of your personal energy persona is the karma that the mirror known as the universe, or the Law of Creation, simply reflects back to you.

When that personal energy persona is *pure authentic you*, then your life is harmonious. That is when you are in the space of BEing your natural self. That purity also affords you the ability to discern the fresh emotions that you are sensing from the environment *in the moment*, and to not be feeling or reacting to any lingering karmic residue from your past. This purity gives you clarity about how you are feeling in *this* moment.

By being able to feel only the feelings that relate to this moment, you afford yourself a very accurate intuitive ability to decide what you want to do. There is untold wisdom behind this ability. It is what affords you the ability to surrender, to trust the intuition of each moment, and to trust that you will intuitively know what choices and actions nurture and support you in the moment—in every moment.

If you were to take a walk in nature and observe a deer grazing in the grass, or a bird chirping in a tree, you would note that there is no contrary thought in those beings as to what they are doing. They are just genuinely being themselves without any inauthentic thought or belief. They are completely present in the moment. They're comfortable in their own skin. And to relate to this as *you, pure authentic you*—that pure space within you that has been there all the time—you cannot erase it. You can either be connected to it, or disconnected from it.

That pure authentic space within you is the signature vibration of your soul. It is the energetic equivalent of the seed vibrations of your own being. It is the source vibration of your dreams coming true. Your heart and your soul are the energetic foundation of your being. All of your karma is riding on top of that foundation.

When the only energy radiating from your personal energy persona is from that pure heart and soul space, then the choice or action available in the moment can be easily weighed with that inner purity. That makes it easier to know which choices and actions are in closer alignment with that pure authentic you. The ego is off the hook in trying to figure out the right path by doing some kind of mental gymnastics. The heart and soul are providing the answers in the moment by creating an energetic vibration of the pure authentic idea of who you really are.

To understand your ability to become pure is to come to terms with every aspect of your being. You can see in all the faces of humanity a reflection of how you see yourself. All the possibilities you can see reflected in the many faces of humanity are the myriad identities you can have within yourself. Any judgment on the face of humanity is a judgment of some aspect of yourself, because in truth the potentiality of you living out any archetype or paradigm is completely and totally possible. Your mind can harbor any thought or belief it wants. You have the potential of preferring any of those possibilities yourself.

The universe itself is not biased at all. The choice exists on the table for you to fulfill, or not fulfill, whatever it is that you despise in humanity, such as the faces of the ones you do not unconditionally accept now. For you, it might be the faces of terrorists. To the terrorists, it might be the faces of infidels. To those who see themselves as "righteous," it might be the faces of those they see as "sinners."

What do you see in humanity that you despise and reject? Imagine yourself playing out *that* role. The universe would fulfill it equally for you too. The universe fulfills all requests with equal vigor. All choices have a merit of one. To the universe, no choice carries an elevated weight. To understand this principle affords you the permission to be your own creator of heaven, to be the savior, the healer, the visionary of the future. The game-changer.

When you understand that the universe is truly unbiased, it affords *you* the permission to be the seed of heaven for humanity, the seed for the reform of our collective systems. Economic, educational, agricultural, medical, societal. On what systems has your life path been centered up to now? On which aspects of life were your core lessons based? During your entire life you have been preparing for this next chapter that is unfolding in your life now.

To come to terms with the many different faces of humanity is to come to terms with them as merely being the choices of that infinite potential of human nature personified in any individual. If there is a person who actually chose those things you despise, to the universe there is no foul. To the universe it is exactly no different than whatever *you* asked the universe to reflect back to you. Nobody has ever broken a karmic law. But if you were to observe people you considered "sinners," from your perspective you might say: "No, that is taboo. That is not desired. That is evil. That is wrong. That is shadow consciousness."

All of those judgments are a projection of what you believe and what you think. It is a mental projection of your own personal imprinting. To understand your imprinting is to follow your life history, the family and culture of your origin into which you were born, and to follow the belief systems that were instilled in your mental and emotional upbringing.

To truly become a king is to be able to transcend all of that. In order for you to be king, in your own kingdom, you need to feel absolute permission to carry out your own inner inspirations. With no hesitations. None. So how do you go about doing that? Would you let go of all judgment of yourself? How would you do that? Well, observe your life and look at your preferences, and then imagine the opposite. Or if you're really bold, live the opposite. A really simple way to do that is to look at how you live your life. You can start discovering your subconscious biasing by changing your preferences.

When we have a subconscious mental imprint, it can hide from our own awareness. Oftentimes others will be able to see traits and attributes in us before we even become cognizant of them ourselves. To bring these inner, subconscious imprints out into the open is to challenge your preferences openly. A simple way to start is to choose just a single room in your home. This simple example has little impact outside of your own personal life. It is a "safe" place to practice these principles, risking only a rather small impact on your life. And it only affects a single room in your house. I mean, it doesn't relate to any other aspect of your life.

So, imagine you are walking into your bedroom now. Where are your clothes? Are they all hung up in a neat row? Are they layered in a chest of drawers folded up nice and proper? Or are they laying on the floor, and you need to wade through them to get to the other side of the room?

In order to learn the nature of your karmic impression, take that preference and experience the total opposite of it. In other words, if you walk into your bedroom and your clothes are all put away, then get them out and throw them on the floor, and leave them there. And if you walk into your bedroom and the clothes are scattered on the floor, fold them up, hang them up, and bring order to the chaos. Whether or not you carry out this or a similar example, you are provided with a perfect opportunity to observe your preferences. As you go to create the opposite condition in your room, and you feel a strong emotional reaction, then you are emotionally motivated for a particular preference. Since there's a strong emotional reaction, the reason why you are having that preference is to preserve a sense of value that you were taught, rather than what you would have chosen.

Oftentimes, when we are raised, we are taught to value a particular preference, and as children we are taught to honor those same values. This type of behavior can be passed down from generation to generation without a genuine discovery of one's true preference. The universe itself does not have any bias; if we were taught a preference (regardless of what we wanted) and we are still honoring that preference, then we are simply perpetuating the preferences of our parents, and we do not genuinely know what we prefer.

This type of preference played itself out during the 1960s when the hippies were protesting on university campuses, and on one side was the hippie ideology where things should be open, and free, and unstructured. Like the clothes on the floor. And on the other side of that interaction was the ideology of authority, saying, "Keep in line and maintain orderly conduct." "Keep the clothes orderly and proper."

And so the polarity of these interactions is the polarity of karma. Neither preference contains elevated value overall. It is our own bias that brings the seeming "karmic penalty" to our experiences. Both sides reside in the polarity of the possibility of our human experience. If we accept that observation, we can simply call it a spectrum of choices, or perceiving one's own preferences from the perspective of a spectrum of choices in any arena of one's life.

Another example would be to imagine a pendulum standing still. The pendulum is located in the center. It is neither left nor right. And if you draw that pendulum up to one side, let's say the right side, at that far right position you can imagine an *iconic* sense of power, the *image* of being powerful. This might be the person wearing a three-piece suit and driving a luxury sports car. Or someone attending an executive meeting. Or a person living in a big house, or in a mansion. This is an extravagant iconic display of power. From this perspective, it is the *iconic* identification with power.

Now, if we bring the pendulum back to center it is located neither left nor right, so then it is neither "good" nor "bad," and we draw it up to the far left position this time. And this time we observe a transient, or a homeless person, living under a bridge. They don't have many possessions to hold onto. There's no iconic attachment at all. Indeed, there is no sense of personal power. From this perspective, there can be a very strong longing for these things, but in truth there isn't any *icon* that holds the identity of power.

In both of these examples the participant is karmically stuck, in a single sense of self. A single idea of self to which they are attached. Both the person wearing the three-piece suit and the transient are stuck in a single sense of themselves. They are each other's karmic shadow. They represent the other side of the karmic spectrum for each other.

The opposite side of the pendulum represents the shadow side of each person. Either position involves being karmically stuck because on the right side (which represents the iconic display of power), if anything happens to the icon, the perception of power is tarnished, it is threatened. So in truth, it is very vulnerable to outside influences.

Yet the homeless person may not have a single icon of power, to live life so vulnerably as to have a sense of uncertainty in all of one's possessions. That would make creating an established platform of expression much more difficult. The creation of lasting effect is in jeopardy on the left side of the pendulum's swing.

When our sense of power is personified through the icons in our life, whatever happens to those icons ultimately affects how we "see" ourselves. Since we have identified with those power icons, whatever happens to those icons reflects upon our own sense of personal power.

To take the necessary steps to becoming a king is to look at and observe all of those spectrums of choices that exist in our human experience, and to notice all of the people who are deciding on their preferences and choices, and who are then fulfilling them. Karmically, the universe is mirroring those preferences back to them. They are using the same principles of creation as we are using. The universe has no bias on what is preferred. Karmically, either side of any spectrum of choice is just as valid as the opposite side of the spectrum.

To become diligent with your thoughts and emotions, and to clean out any incongruent aspects within your personal energy persona, is to move more into alignment with your soul's dream of your life being fulfilled. That is the journey itself. As long as there's flow there, as long as there's incremental change moving you more into alignment with that pure authentic idea within you, the dream is being fulfilled. There's never a moment when the journey is over.

To enjoy Heaven on Earth now is to enjoy the here and now, the perfection of the here and the now. You don't have to follow your story through to completion in order to find heaven. Heaven can only exist here and now. Your ability, or inability, to experience this is directly related to your purity.

When you become pure, you will truly be living Heaven on Earth. And the way to become pure is to have unconditional love for any person who has chosen any polarity of any spectrum, period! How would it feel if that truly happened? Imagine you step into an elevator, and then as you go up or down, the elevator stops at a floor and somebody gets on. No matter who that somebody is, you say, "But of course you can choose whatever you have chosen."

If they are a reflection of your own karmic shadows, you don't drop into judgment of them, creating a sense that they made "wrong choices." Because if you see them as having made "wrong choices" then it is also possible in your own beliefs for *you* to make wrong choices.

To the universe, it is all a moot point. To any request it always responds the same. "But of course." The mirror doesn't care. And that which we might perceive as a "bad" choice has existed forever, and will exist forevermore. We are living on a planet where people are loaded to the hilt with karma. But of course, this is a possibility in the many, many paradigms playing out now on our planet. Once you can embody this simple principle of purity, then you can genuinely live as a king in your own kingdom, and that kingdom is actually Heaven on Earth.

Heaven on Earth is a completely inclusive space. To become pure about all of the choices of all of the spectrums of our human condition—to be able to accept them as if we chose them for ourselves, and to have that kind of innocent acceptance—affords us the opportunity in every moment to make any choice that our heart and soul give us without judgment.

What's important about this is that when your ego and your mind are pure and in a state of peace, and when your heart and soul throw out an idea, then your mind can recognize it as being from your heart and soul. There is no need to quantify it, or vet it, or check it by your ego. It is already vetted. It is already approved. It is in perfect alignment with who you are. No second thought necessary. No critical thinking necessary. It is the spontaneous fulfillment of the heart's inspiration of the moment. To be able to recognize that the idea has clearly come from your heart is all that is required for you take action on it.

Forgiveness and compassion are the power tools needed to genuinely build a kingdom in which you can live with a sense of joy, fulfillment, accomplishment, and genuine happiness. You experience happiness because there's flow in your life and you are fulfilling the inspiration of your heart and soul.

All the while your ego is choosing joy every day. Your heart, your soul, and your ego are all in joy because your dreams are being fulfilled. That is the authentic vibration of heaven. When you can personify that vibration because you've released all judgment of any human choice *ever*, then you can be at peace no matter who gets on the elevator. You can remain in that place of peace.

In that place of peace where you are quiet and at rest, you can capture the impulse of your heart in each moment. Since you have no attachment as to whether your clothes are hanging up neatly in the closet or if they're laying on the floor, you don't have any judgment of which choice is "right" and which choice is "wrong." You don't have a subconscious impulse that places judgment on your own inspiration, because in truth, every choice available to us has a merit of one. Every image you can show a mirror has a merit of one. The mirror doesn't effort any more to reflect a vibrantly colored, high-resolution image back to you, nor does it do so for a scratchy black-and-white image. In other words, no matter what choice you make the universe fulfills it with equal merit.

You get the idea. Your life has progressed to this moment in time. Your past reflects a story of your relationship with the elements of your life outside of you, and how your ego has managed the people and circumstances outside of you. To break that up with forgiveness and compassion within your own personal energy persona is like polishing a mirror. It is polishing the mirror so that the clear image of your dream can land on it, and be reflected back to you perfectly. When the mirror is pure and your heart and soul are living in unconditional love, that is the thing itself. The mirror gladly reflects unconditional love back to you. That is the doorway to heaven itself.

To know that you have permission, unconditional permission now, to live your dreams fulfilled is the key to owning your own personal power. You have unconditional permission now, just like everybody on the planet has unconditional permission to choose any choice they want. The universe truly has no bias.

You are innocent. You are free. The canvas has been wiped clean. You write the screenplay. You are the director. When you honor the genuinely *authentic* preference that you have within you, you are making the choice that keeps you in alignment—that keeps you in purity in alignment—with unconditional love, where you forgive yourself unconditionally. You understand that karmically no image shown to the mirror ever violates the reflection. In truth, nobody has ever violated a karmic law. It is impossible. Since it is impossible, you have permission to choose whatever you want in this moment and in every moment, as does every other consciousness who's living in this space.

The floodgates are now open. The keys are in your heart. You've always held the keys to the kingdom. No person outside of you can ever take those away. You always have permission. You always have the solution, the resolution. Nobody can take away your authentic vibration. The ego doesn't have that kind of influence, as much as it would like to think so sometimes. Trust that your dream, *your* dream, is handcrafted for you. Sometimes that dream can seem strange to the ego's relationship with the past.

I say this as an author, because during the first couple of decades of my living on this planet, if you had walked up to me and asked, "Are you an author?" I would have laughed. But here I am today, writing books. When I honor that by actually being an author, and as I write these words right now, I am fulfilling my heart's impression in the moment. And today I will have fulfilled all three elements of who I am—my heart, soul and mind—and what I saw as a possibility.

By honoring that authentic impulse, I am living in a place of peace, a place of deep fulfillment, and in a deep sense of joy that I'm actually honoring my potential and fulfilling my purpose. It doesn't matter what step of the journey I'm on in this moment. I just took action steps on those inspirations and that's it. Period. Done. "I'll have the ice cream please. Make it a double scoop."

When you give yourself permission to live the life you truly and genuinely enjoy, then your reflection in the sea of humanity is that of a king living in a kingdom where the city is vibrant and healthy. Where the city is full of art, passionate expression, dance, and song. Where our choices encompass healthy food, clean air, water, and earth. The valley has turned green partially because you live there. The choices of your heart brought prosperity to the environment in which you live. The valley has turned green because of you fulfilling your heart and listening to its inspiration.

Heaven *can* be present on earth. Heaven *is* an inherent vibration within our being that cannot be erased. The pure vibration of heaven is in you now. It exists at your core. It has always been there. It is the most authentic and genuine vibration of the human experience, and it always exists forever within us as a choice vibration that the mirror can reflect back to us.

# Chapter 12

# HEALING YOUR PAST

In order for us to show up as a king in our lives we need to have healed our journey to the kingdom. Kings, prior to having dominion over their country, first had to pass some tests in order to determine whether or not they were worthy. If you look at the structure of a kingdom, you will see that there are lesser positions that must first be filled that ultimately lead to the role of a king becoming king.

In order for you to be able to genuinely and authentically become a king, you need to learn the lessons of the lesser positions that lead to the kingdom. To understand your own mental and emotional imprinting affords you the ability to resolve it and become free of its karmic tendencies. The way you do this is by observing mental and emotional patterning within your own persona.

"Well, how do I discover mental and emotional patterning within my personal energy persona?" Let me give you an example! This example relates to a mental imprint within my own psyche as it relates to how to acquire something that I want. My father grew up in a poor household. I know his parents must have told him, "Look, Son, if you want something, you're going to have to make it yourself." In other words, "We can't afford it. If you want something in your life you're going to have to make it yourself."

And so my father got really good at learning how to make things. He taught himself how to make all sorts of things. For instance, he made a fold-out camping trailer for his truck long before such a thing was commonplace. He built a fishing boat. He crafted canoes. He made most everything he wanted with his own hands, because that was the way he was given permission to show up. He had a propensity to solve a problem with a singular approach, which was to make it yourself if you wanted it.

The above is an example of mental posturing. So, so what? That was my dad. So what? What was the big deal? Actually, it was a huge deal for me. I first recognized the mental imprint it had left on me when I wanted to acquire an air compressor. When I decided I wanted an air compressor, I didn't even think to go out and buy one. Rather, I started gathering the parts. I got a tank. Then I found a motor. I located a compressor. I got my hands on some valves and gauges. You see, because of my mental imprinting, I couldn't just go out and *buy* one. I *had to make it.* Dad passed his imprinting onto me, and so I couldn't just buy an air compressor. The only thought that arose out of my inspiration was that I had to make it!

As I got older, I didn't live anywhere near the poverty level in which my dad grew up. Sure, he held a good job, a secure government job, and we had a roof over our house and food on the table. However, especially with a large family to take care of, financially times were often tight. But we never talked about it, though I saw the stress of money written all over my mother's face, mostly appearing as emotional desperation, or anxiety. But we never openly talked about it as a family.

Consequently, on an emotional level, I experienced a big trigger around money. I realized that in order for me to become a king in my own kingdom, I needed to be able to convert my inspiration into actual outcomes, outcomes that were larger in scale. In other words, in order for me to be able to manifest creation at the level that my soul can inspire me to do, my ability to manifest these things, or not, will determine whether I can operate as a king of my own kingdom or not. I also realized that if I experience mental and emotional imprinting in my psyche, then I won't be able to have an untethered expression of my soul. There will be some dogmatic reaction, some dogmatic patterning, some dogmatic subconscious preferences that will keep me in the old story, in the old paradigm.

In order for me to truly and genuinely be king in my own kingdom (in other words, for me to live my life encompassing the very idea, the very dream, that my soul can conjure up for me) is to have a clear pallet, is to have a clean canvas, is to have an energetically pure personal energy persona that is free of mental and emotional patterning from the past.

When I can afford that for my soul's inspiration, all possibilities are real. All ideas can actually be fulfilled. That's when my life starts to expand. That's when I'm going to need to hold on, because the expression of the vision of my soul will always transcend what my ego could have conjured up. And the better I get at following my heart and soul's inspiration, the greater effect I can have in each passing day. Consciousness seeks expansion. And the consciousness of my own soul will expand into my everyday life.

By cleansing my mental and emotional patterning I'm preparing myself to genuinely and authentically be a king in my own kingdom. But what would that look like? It would look like me having inspiration from my heart in the moment, an idea sent to me arriving from my heart on what action I can take in that moment. I don't take it up into my head. I don't rationalize it. I don't second-guess it. I don't quantify it. I don't give it a critical eye. I just do it. I just do it without hesitation, because none of my mental or emotional patterning is there to be triggered, and thus I am free.

When you have resolved the mental and emotional imprinting in your own subconscious, there is nothing left there about which to react. This allows the perfect action available in the moment to actually be chosen and followed without any subconscious imprinting getting in the way. It allows genuine freedom to fulfill it in the most graceful way possible in each moment.

But without cleansing our old imprints, what will often happen is that our heart and soul will give us such a big idea that will, in turn, trigger mental and emotional re-actions that re-start the patterning from our past. Once that happens, we move from thinking with our hearts to thinking with our heads, and all bets are off. Chances are it's not going to happen. The idea will be gone. Our dreams stop.

The path to creation is curtailed. The inspiration will have no effect on our future.

Genuinely acting as a king in my own kingdom means becoming perfectly still, to be quiet and still in each moment, enough that I am cognizant of the fresh inspiration of my heart and soul in that moment. And it doesn't mean I can't be playing sports, or cranking up the music, or dancing around my living room. You can still live any kind of life you want to live. But to be still by becoming cleansed of your mental and emotional patterning affords you the ability to capture the vast majority of your heart's inspiration. Whereas if you stop thinking from the arena of your heart, and your thinking moves up into your head and from a place of ego, that's when the patterning kicks in. That is when you start missing the mark. You stop firing on all cylinders. You start rationalizing the inspiration that your heart and soul have for you in that day, in that hour, in that minute—so it's missed time.

It is a very powerful thing to cleanse the emotional and mental imprinting of your past. So when you have an idea that might require the acquisition of something that you want, such as in my example of an air compressor, you go out and you buy it. And you instantly move on to the next step, amplifying how much you can accomplish in the moment.

In fact, maybe you start a business that fulfills your inspiration. And you hire the people that you need to help run the shop. You start thinking at a much bigger level, and you transcend the imprinting of your past. That's the whole point behind the king being able to give your soul carte blanche freedom, untethered freedom to inspire the vision of what your life can become in this moment now.

All that the ego has to do when it receives inspiration is to fulfill that inspiration. Make the call. Sign the form. Send the email. Order the package. Create the web site. Make it happen. The ego makes it happen, all the while choosing joy throughout the day. "Yes, I'll have the caramel ice cream." "Yes, I'll go for a run after work." "Yes, I'll learn how to garden." Or whatever you're genuine inspiration involves.

That's when the power of a king—*you* acting as a powerful king—can channel the inspiration of your soul into actions during the day while you are choosing your own authentic personal preferences. At the end of the day you will have been acting as a king in a kingdom—because that will be exactly what you are, a king—fulfilling the inspiration of *your* heart and *your* soul, and the vision of your dreams.

When you can get good at that, all things become possible. Your wand starts working again, and a quickening starts to happen. To genuinely understand the idea of what it means to be a Citizen King is to genuinely give yourself permission to press eject on the DVD player of the story of your life that you've been living up to this moment. Letting go of any attachments to the past. Genuinely giving yourself permission to clean out any mental and emotional posturing from the past, and affording you any genre with which you choose to replace it. The adventurer. Or the composer. The writer. The singer. The dancer. The gardener. The farmer. All the genres become available from your place of purity.

When you understand what it means to be a *Citizen King*, you genuinely give yourself permission to choose the exact genre, the right DVD, and the perfect storyline that would most make you happy as you fulfill the inspiration of your heart and soul. That's when you step into the kingdom with boldness, with a sense of power. Power that has grace as its wake. Power that has love as its fuel. Power that has absolute effect because of its purity. When you have accomplished that, then you *are* a *Citizen King* walking around on this beautiful planet experiencing your own personal kingdom within.

# Chapter 13

# IMAGINATION
# MAKES IT HAPPEN

The village is at ease. Today is the announcement of your vision for the kingdom. Everyone is glad to gather again. The blue skies and crisp summer morning have everyone feeling the delight. You are about to read your proclamation to the kingdom. This is your vision of the kingdom living in peace, love, joy and balance. You have mastered that, and this vision which you will share today will bring even more of the kingdom into opulence, abundance on all levels.

Imagine a kingdom where everyone is tuned in to their own intuition, trusting the feeling of this now. That endless stream of emotional information, affording the most harmonious decision in every moment. Weighing the vibration of the choices, with the authentic signature vibration of their dream. An energetic snapshot of your overall vibe, if you were to be fulfilling the dream. This always produces peace, joy and happiness.

Oh sure, there will be ups and downs. There is always more to learn about this life that we are living during this chapter of our human mythology. What is our story? What are we manifesting for ourselves and future generations? Getting clear there tends to bring an even bigger dream into your vision. When you start honoring the vision, and creating flow toward fulfilling your dream, you capture the feeling of compassion behind your actions. Your heart is connected to every heart on the planet. When you start to follow the inspiration of your heart you see the direction of your life move into a place of service to others, for an open heart cannot consciously bring pain to another. As every king follows the inspiration of their own heart, our actions move to a place of compassion and understanding—ending the cycle of violence toward one another. By shifting the guidance of our lives out of our ego and into our hearts we break the old story, the old pattern, of oppression and dominance. When we have created a kingdom where the inhabitants are following their hearts, we have created a community that is centered in love. By living in this love we are creating Heaven on Earth.

To truly be able to leverage our authentic power is to learn how to value and trust our own imagination. It will be through our imagination that the vision of heaven arrives for us. That dream factory that is within each of us now contains our own ability to engage our imagination with a sense of lucidness that is empty of motive or attachment. Guided by our own authentic preferences, it can bring an idea that is bigger than our mind alone could create.

When we can show up in that openness, we can capture any idea. The power of an imagination is the ability to capture inspiration in its most original vibration. It is the seed scene to our storyline for our life now—a picture of us enjoying life, just as it is.

There is an attitude portrayed in the movie, *Alice in Wonderland*, that conveys the idea of constantly stretching our imagination. The notion went like this. Before breakfast, think of six things you believe are impossible to create in your own life. This mental stretch is a great way to open up and expand our ability to imagine. This is scrubbing the screen clean, so to speak, that your movie can play out on.

When we are karmically laden, we already have a story playing out on our screen, the screen of our mind. It is like having our old story loaded in the projector, and then loading our new vision in with it as well. The old story dilutes and pollutes the images of our new inspiration. Like that preloaded film of our past, our subconscious motivations can hinder our ability to capture a truly unique idea. The clarity of our karmic canvas or screen is a result of how much of our past we have resolved. To be able to cleanse the old energies out of our own personal energy persona is to allow the new idea to abide within ourselves in a clean and pure place.

When we have resolved our past, it allows the purity of our inspiration to fulfill its image on the screen without any distortion from our past. To get ourselves energetically pure is to carry out the deep cleaning needed within our own personal energy persona. This is where compassion and forgiveness are key to creating a deep cleanse; they literally reprogram the storyline of each individual.

When we have energetic elements of unresolved consciousness present in our karmic profile, they energetically create a momentum of more of the same. The old energy present in us can attract the old story to play out again. To be able to create a new paradigm is to have no energy contrary to the new inspiration within our own karma. Thus, we are allowing the new inspiration to be the only script of what we will be choosing and acting on in our future.

To truly transcend the old paradigm that is playing out, and thus capture the seed of a miracle, is to be able to receive the inspiration in the moment, and hold it without diluting or polluting it with mental, emotional or spiritual karmic residues. Until you can live there, you have residual karma of the past, present in your consciousness. No worries. Karma is the paint on the canvas itself. It is the paint of life itself. The richness of our experience is the byproduct of our karmic journey. And if you look closely enough, you can see that consciousness is playing out a belief and feeling. Karmic fulfillment. To avoid it is to extend it. As always, the choice is yours. There is no wrong choice. All choices are fulfilled with equal merit.

To expand your imagination is to become more aware of your own karmic patterns. These are mental and emotional re-actions that crop up throughout your day. When you watch movies or read blogs or commentary, observe how your thoughts and feelings change. Catch those moments when a frequent pattern starts up again in your daily consciousness.

It's like having a bloated version of an old operating system loaded on a computer, which makes the computer run slower than slow! This is the equivalent of having many re-active patterns in your daily interaction with others, and then being able to catch yourself when a re-action starts up again. It is when you can sense a shift in your feelings and thoughts, and then consciously choose a different re-action to the thoughts and feelings in the moment, that you can choose a new outcome. It is the ability to be able to preserve the energetic signature of your dreams, and to clear up all of the subprograms that are running in your mind, bogging you down, and diluting the purity of the vision.

If you are truly going to walk as a king amongst your kingdom, you would do well to have a vivid view of your dreams as if they have already come true. When your dreams occupy a larger and larger part of your everyday thoughts and feelings, then you are on your journey as a king fulfilling all aspects of your kingdom.

So what do you prefer to do? What food do you like the best? Where is your dream home located? What color is it? What does it look like if you were to drive up to it now? Spending the time to polish the dream anchors it in your thoughts. The more time you spend refining what you prefer, the easier your choices in the moment become. And it becomes easier to know which choices will move you toward your dreams. To honor your dreams with your choices and actions grants you permission to act as a king in your own kingdom.

You are a soul personified. A soul by itself could be seen as a generic actor of sorts, a soul personified as the personality behind every human being. Behind every human choice and action, there is a soul playing out the karmic storyline. Your soul could be playing out any other storyline similar to that which any other human being is playing out right now on this planet. Or it could be playing out something completely different, both "good" and "bad." The actors are never held in contempt of the story of their script in the end.

We are all souls playing out our own particular life story. Whatever our story is, it is incidental to our soul presence. Our soul is the source of life that feeds our body and makes our heart beat. Since our soul can play out any paradigm in this collective story playing out in humanity right now it could, therefore, be playing out any other storyline too.

How many of us have karmic train wrecks in our past? No matter how bad the story, karmically you are free and clear. No problem. You are good to go. The universe does not put forth any requirements for how you live out your future. Karmically we have to give *ourselves* permission to fulfill the very imprint of our heart and soul. We need to have a vision that transcends the existing paradigm of the collective, as well as the personal permission to bring it about. This trait is what produces Gandhis, Buddhas, Christs. This trait is in you now. Find it. Live it. Love it! The dream is there waiting just for you.

Trust in *your* journey. Trust in *your* story. You are the actor in this play of your life. What are your preferences? What is your joy? What makes you happy? Do that! To imagine a kingdom where everyone is fulfilled is to live a satisfying life. Eating healthy food. Taking in clean air, water and earth. Nature is thriving all over the planet. Life is abundant. It is a kingdom filled with its own riches. It is *you* playing out the passion of your life.

To be able to bring about the new idea of what a healthy kingdom looks like, is to give ourselves permission to create a whole new possibility with our own inspiration. So much of our culture does not afford us genuine personal sovereignty. The new kings will be the ones that are inspired by their heart and soul to fulfill the inspiration that brings a better sense of personal freedom and sovereignty to our culture.

This inspiration will come from within ourselves. It will take on many new ideas. Citizens who have spent their whole lifetimes up until now, working in a particular field or industry, will be inspired to start a new model of their vocation. They will create a new model of how it operates, often moving the industry from a monolithic pyramid structure toward a honeycomb structure. This will bring new structures into place that provide more choices for humanity and that are resistant to deceit or control, that honor the citizen's place in this new chapter of our human story.

In other words, so many of our resources are fulfilled through just a few corporations, which are monolithic-type structures. And the new paradigm will create a model that is based on many smaller, more flexible, resilient, and reproducible structures.

Veteran bankers will devise new banking systems. People working in the energy sector will discover new ideas for creating more independence and freedom in that sector, generating many more choices for how our basic necessities are supplied. Improved agricultural practices and better health will follow as well.

The idea of a Citizen King is about all of us walking in step, yet following the beat within our own hearts. A legion of new kings, fulfilling the inspiration of their own hearts, will be able to step out of the story of their past, and yet act like powerful new kings in a free and robust new kingdom.

To take on this new role is to grant yourself permission to act and move in powerful new directions. Understand that you are here to do just that. You are the souls who will bring the new inspirations into creation. You are the souls who will bring a new sense of freedom to the masses. Trust in your part of this dynamic process. Trust in your purpose.

When you create a new movie with a new story, you hire actors. The storyline of a movie typically has many roles available to be played out. At the beginning phase of creating a movie, actors gather to audition for their parts in the movie. They don't know what role they will eventually play. In that regard, they are innocent. Whether they are assigned the role of the saint or the sinner, either way, right now, they are just an actor applying for a role, just as you are playing out your karmic role right now. Whatever story your past has to share, you are simply a soul playing out your part in this movie.

The storyline of our collective consciousness is changing right now by those souls who take action on their new inspiration. If you are reading this book right now, *your* soul is here to start a new paradigm for humanity, based on your experience of the past and your inspiration of the future. You have permission to do just that. You are part of the method of change for all of humanity.

To be able to honor your own immense potential, you must be the actor that plays out the role of a king living in his or her own kingdom, exactly as you prefer. The universe gladly fulfills it. The lamp in the projector does not have any concern as to the nature of the film that is loaded into the projector. Every soul or actor can play out any storyline it chooses.

So what's in *your* projector? You are the director, producer, writer, and actor of this play called your life. What image can you hold energetically? What feelings and thoughts can you play out in this script that you have written for yourself? Can you see beyond the current collective storyline, and reach into that infinite well, called your imagination, and pull out a dream of Heaven on Earth, personified through you, as you?

# Chapter 14

# CASTING THE VISION

You are human consciousness personifying [INSERT YOUR NAME HERE]. You can be living out any script now, acting like a king. By honoring *your* soul, *you* could create a whole new industry. Or the curtains close to a standing ovation of your first screenplay enactment. You cure cancer. You sign the papers and the construction of the new healing center begins. You have effect. You are aware of the vision, and can capture it, and sustain it in its original purity from the first moment you received it. The pure dream.

And then as you bring your awareness to it, you bring along your karmic propensities too. The nature of your particular preferences. And always, the universe obliges. To become a Citizen King is to be able to recognize that the image is from your higher self. It is to capture the pure image, and then weigh all choices in the moment, based on the one that is closer in frequency, thus moving energetically toward purity. When purity arrives, the dream is fulfilled, as there will be no other energy present.

You can think of the vision of your soul as a never-ending vision of your dreams coming true. Like a beacon broadcasting the image of your dream. A pure energetic image of it. The gift from your soul. When the ego/mind can make it a preference in the moment, then there is progress toward purity itself. When the king is pure, nothing is out of reach, because the soul is the only energetic presence, having absolute effect in what the mirror reflects back to you as your experience. And the truth will set you free.

What the ego needs to understand in order to genuinely be free is that your consciousness is always present. It cannot be destroyed. As such, you are free now. You are safe now. You are impossible to destroy. A soul personified as you, the human being. Your soul was present before you were born, and will continue on after your body dies.

In other words, imagine you are an actor on the stage of a live performance, known as *your life playing out.* Then imagine stopping that play, with you walking over to you as the actor, and telling yourself the following: "The actor, which is your soul, will never die. The script you are living out now will never be playing out a part where your consciousness ceases to exist. Your consciousness progresses after this body is gone."

Get clear about that, and you will relax. When that happens, you will be able to embody your soul much better. In that peace, from karmic purity, you are living in the moment, the way your soul dreamed it. Pure authentic you. Innocent in every moment. No matter the choice. You are forgiven, released and free, now and always, as you are a point of presence of human consciousness. As such, you are a point of presence in the hologram of consciousness. This understanding gives you permission to trust the Divine approval that your choices have for you, now, and in every moment.

It is in that place of total trust of the divinity of you living out your life as you choose that innocence is recognized, and the soul has the ability to totally craft the energetic idea of this moment now—thus choosing what you are attracting to yourself as you walk your life path. It is you, a *new human living* on this wonderful planet Earth.

So surrender to your dream as the perfect script for your life. In that place of total acceptance and relaxation also comes a deep sense of satisfaction, and a sense of fulfillment towards one's life potential. Give your soul the reigns to paint any picture of your life to create a Heaven on Earth. Give yourself that personal sovereignty to choose as your heart and soul inspires you to. Period.

To embody the vision of our soul is to become a vessel of purity. It is to be able to embody the light. This affords us every arena of karmic expression. Every paradigm becomes a viable option. The less we hold on to our attachments, the more powerfully we can make choices in this and every moment. The closer we live in the light, the more manifestation options we have in each passing moment now. The more we live in the light, the more power we give to our souls to manifest through ourselves.

Kings can tap that field of infinite potential, and start to wrap a framework around it, knowing the power of a single idea, and then knowing how to bring it about. To be able to embody the precise vibration of the dream, and then weigh the choices of every moment against it, affords the vision of our soul to become manifest—through us, and as us. It is conscious creation itself.

An example of living more embodied in our own light is to move our director's chair toward the light bulb in the movie projector. In the past, our ego was engaged with the story of the movie on the screen. Yet the light from the movie projector can play any movie. The light represents the infinite possibilities of consciousness itself. Yet the story of any one movie has a karmic tone to it. A karmic signature. A static imprint of what the story is about. It was a karmic momentum, playing out as a collage of re-active karmic tendencies, each one having an energetic component in our own personal energy persona.

To be a Citizen King is to be able to live in total peace in each moment of every day, so that any energetic impulse of the moment, seeded by our own soul, resolves any seeming requirements in the moment. Karmically, nothing is required. That liberty is largely why we all went so far inside the collective darkness. We chose to take the journey into the darkness to understand a broader and deeper understanding of our human nature. To master the art of BEing human. In all the paradigms possible.

But here we are now, able to be present in this moment, and able to fulfill the energetic signatures flowing from our innermost selves. We are taking actions, one after another, completely based on the highest vibrational inspiration available in each and every moment. To be able to dial that in, for our own authentic self without a second thought, is to present the storyline of our soul, front and center, in this ever-present moment.

For our soul to feed us the inspiration that will return us to the light is the journey of all of humanity; all souls return to the light, the source of all creation. For *you* to be taking that very journey now, in *this* lifetime, is to experience the greatest shift in consciousness in a single lifetime. To come from so far in the darkness, back into the light within such a relatively short period of time, makes for an epic adventure. To trust in *your* soul's inspiration, affords a path back to the light that makes it all possible. The inspiration of the soul shows you the way.

This provides our ego with freedom from responsibility as it relates to "having to figure it out." We do not have to *think* our way through our life, but rather, we can *feel* our way through it in each and every moment, once we have cleared out the old residual karma from our subconscious. It is in experiencing the feelings that are present in each moment that provide the Divine guidance of our life path. "Just in time" guidance, so to speak. The ego is off the hook. It only takes action on the inspiration, and chooses those things that it finds enjoyable. Like when you open the menu in a restaurant, and you see glazed caramel salmon listed. "That's what I'd like to eat for dinner." Done! "And I think I'll have a shot of whiskey on the side." Done! As *you* choose. Carte blanche.

The universe has no bias of its own. It has been fulfilling the karmic signatures of humans who have been living out their karmic journey for eons. Here it is now, responding to your energetic signature, right now. And now. And now. To be in alignment with your soul's idea, or signature vibration of the dream of your life being fulfilled, is to present only that idea to the mirror of the universe, which gladly fulfills it. Heaven on Earth. You living as a Citizen King. Carte blanche. As *you* prefer. The creator incarnate.

The question becomes, how much personal sovereignty can you embody in your life right now? How completely free of fear and guilt can you be when choosing your preferences? Who are you to have dominion over the thoughts and feelings that are expressing within you now?

To be able to detect the signature vibration of your soul, and to act on it in the moment, is to embody your soul's vision of what is possible for you, and for humanity as a whole. You are living as the king that you truly are in your own kingdom that is within you now. You are completely expressing your vision in the moment without hesitation or regard. Your ego doesn't have to vet your dreams, as there is no need for approval. Your dreams are pre-approved, and handcrafted for your enjoyment. So enjoy the dream, fill your cup to overflowing with your vision, and live your enlightened life.

Living in peace is the result of being able to purify yourself. The karmic imprinting that we are experiencing is a running history reflective of our own past. Every energetic element within our own being has a history to it. A storyline of our own personal past, which describes the accumulation of karmic experiences.

To be able to be a king is to resolve all of that energetically. In the process of doing that, you become intuitive about how you feel in the moment, in the now. When you can learn to trust that intuition, without worry or concern, you are standing at the doorway to freedom. If you are not a free king, then you are not a king. So be free.

Being a Citizen King means looking at your community through the eyes of the dream. The vision of life living in harmony with itself. That is the place of nature. That is the place of Heaven.

The other aspect of being a king is to create, without hesitation or question. When the vision of the dream is big, start taking big steps. Trust in the intuition of this now moment to tell you what to choose in this moment; giving your soul that kind of liberty over your own thoughts ensures the shortest path to your dreams coming true.

In that ongoing journey that takes place day after day, the mind, the ego, chooses those thoughts that brings it joy! "Let's go for a walk out in nature today." "I'll have the ice cream." "I want to extend my vacation." "I'll attend that concert tonight." And the universe responds back with, "As you so choose. As you wish. Your wish is my command!"

When all of these scenarios line up, heaven is found within the joy of the harmony of mind, heart and soul walking in step with each other. When each citizen is living in that place, then peace is found on Earth, and the karmic tragedies are resolved, raising the vibration of the whole kingdom.

So what is *your* role in it? What do *you* love to do? Get clear about that. Get that vision in super-high definition, crisp and clean.

And know that residing in that theme is your own personal heaven. *You*, living *your* dreams. Pure authentic you!

When the purity of your own authentic energy is the only reflection of the mirror alone, then *your* soul is driving your life, polishing the karmic lens so that it can pass total purity affords us the power to raise our own consciousness to the soul level. The scope in which the soul operates has no boundary or barrier of any kind. The soul can envision you fulfilling your gift to an ever-larger arena.

When the soul gets to drive, the vision expands. Always. You, the mind, simply keeps immediately executing the impulse of the moment, staying grounded in your body, and focused on the pure vibrations of your dreams. It means being cognizant of the energy behind your choices, and the vibration of your dreams, in their purest form. In that space, the better choice is the choice that vibrates closer to your dream's vibration.

The choice that provides the shortest path to your dreams coming true is laid out before you. By looking at the vibration of each of your choices, and following the one that feels good, you start to move the thinking of your mind toward the arena your soul has in mind for your enjoyment. The more you sharpen the vision of your dreams, the easier the choices become in each passing moment. You simply take steps and choose what you prefer, over and over, ad infinitum.

As you purify your own personal energy persona, your intuition of the moment gets clearer and easier to read. By carrying out the necessary cleansing, you get better at trusting each moment to express what you need to know. The more you can trust yourself, the more peace will show up in your life and in the wake of your choices.

A good way to understand what your purity looks like in this moment of your journey is to simply take a look at your wake, the results of your past decisions. If your life became more integrated by accepting life just the way it was, then your energy became more pure. If your life moved toward separation, you rejected and judged what was happening around you, adding karma to your subconscious. More energy would have been added that, in turn, the mirror of the universe would have reflected back to you, moving you further into darkness.

When we make choices that create separation, we are creating karmic energy within our own personal energy persona. Karmically there is no wrong. You can never break a karmic law. Just start paying more attention. There is a powerful lesson behind every karmic element. Do not be afraid to just feel it. Let it tell you what it is there to tell you. Trust your feelings about it. Learn to understand what your feelings are telling and showing you. The more time you spend in that place, the more you can learn to trust this moment and every moment.

When that trust becomes the reflex of every moment, you set yourself free. You soar with the vision of your life, just as you prefer. When you give yourself permission to take action on any and all of your soul's inspirations, the broader your life vision becomes. How *big* do you want to play? How *bold* do you dare stride? Don't tell me. Tell *you!*

# Chapter 15

# LIVING THE DREAM!

Although this book portrays a king living in the 1800's, it actually doesn't matter which chapter you take from the human storyline of the entire mythology of humanity itself. Imagine the collective story of all of humanity on this planet, with each lifetime playing out in sequential chapters someplace in the book of our human mythology.

You are living a chapter of that book right now. Your life now. What you do with that will decide your story. You are a point of presence of the infinite story of humanity. What inspirations await your desire to fulfill them in you now? What would genuinely make you happy?

Take the time to get clear about that. The projector in your own personal energy persona is seeding the future. Plant the seeds of your inspirations, and take actions to fulfill them, just the steps that you can take today. The rest of the story will wait its turn on the timeline of this life. Your life. As long as you are making steps toward that dream, taking action on the inspiration, you can go to bed feeling fulfilled and genuinely happy *today*.

That is the doorway to Heaven on Earth. Go and live there if you so choose. Perhaps I'll feel your presence there, or you will feel mine. The projector is always running. Your movie is playing out right now. You are a human being living in the current chapter of the human mythology on this planet now. Who were you this day? What will you be remembered for?

The universe will gladly fulfill whatever you load into your karmic energy projector. Scrub the lens of your karmic projector with the cleansers of forgiveness and compassion—for yourself and for all of humanity—so that we can all walk in step with the one beating heart of humanity.

This human paradigm has been playing out for eons on our planet. Our chapter is just that, a chapter. We are always authoring the next sentence karmically with our own energy right now. Being cognizant of that is the advantage point. In every moment of the whole story, we all were the thing itself, playing out the storyline of that individual person in that individual paradigm.

What is your passion in this play? What part of the collective human story gets you the most excited? Where do your talents and abilities shine through? That is the doorway to *your* dreams coming true for you. Honoring your potential and purpose is the key to happiness. To fulfill the desires of your heart and soul is to live the extraordinary life.

This idea is indifferent to whether you are a man or a woman. It doesn't know any differences. Every human on the planet has equal access to this inner knowing, to the process of creation. We all have it in equal measure. It is the process of creation of human consciousness. It doesn't have any bias of its own. The projector doesn't have any preference for the movie you choose. The power in the movie is those heart and soul inspirations that you feed it.

That is the script of your dreams coming true. To follow that inspiration in the moment is the best action that you can take in this ever-present now. To be able to capture the idea, the vision, the scene of what your dream would look like if it has already come true, and then take actions that move toward fulfillment, is the process itself. The only variation is the rate in which it happens.

If you have a lot of old mental and emotional patterning going on, then the rate will not be very responsive. Learning how to improve that, and to actually take the steps to making the dream come true, is the thing itself. It has no concern if it is a masculine mind or a feminine mind receiving the inspiration. Did you capture its authentic essence? Are you comparing all of your choices to its vibration, and then choosing the choices that are closer in resonance with the pure authentic vibration of your inspiration? It is as if you become an impeccable keeper of the authentic vibration of inspiration, a resolution of purity.

The idea of being a Citizen King, granting your heart and soul carte blanche over your own choices and actions, is always a place of power expressed. You are the receptor of the inspiration, and you are the vehicle of its expression. Get the wheels turning and you'll have something to learn about the process along the way.

To know when the idea has come from your heart and soul, and then to capture the purity of your future potential, is the birth of the seed of its creation through you, as you. Get that down to a reflex, and the rules start to melt away. If indeed we are living in a holographic universe, and that hologram is of consciousness expressing itself, then you already have the keys to the kingdom in your hands now, and always.

The only question is, is there any flow happening, and are you expanding that portal of expression? Get those two things down, and you will start creating motion toward your dreams coming true. The better you get at it, the bigger your dreams will become. That is the place of a true Citizen King, where you can be inspired in the moment and know that this inspiration is the *authentic you*. It is a place where you can instantly fulfill the fun action(s) that your inner child has available to it to choose from every single day.

We all have the "Peace on Earth" gene. We all have the dream of what a wonder-full life would look and feel like for ourselves personally. Trust in your role of living as a Citizen King.

What kinds of inspiration and actions get you the most excited? Go and do that. Be careful along the way. Just because you have an "aha" vision doesn't mean you just quit your job and move to who knows where. There is a discipline to living a well-paced life.

But you don't have to wait for your dream to come true to begin living a life you so totally enjoy. You can always start today. Heaven will never be experienced on any other day than today. This day now. Heaven on Earth is found within each one of us, once we unravel the patterning of our past. We are all free to living the life we love. It is our birthright, now and forever. It is understanding the value and the precious gift that you are now. Whether you decide to show up or not is always your choice to make. The projector doesn't care, and it will play any movie you create. So figure out what you really genuinely prefer. And then do that.

Know that you cannot break a karmic law. We are given fierce freedom. Spend it well. May your journey toward becoming your own inner king be filled with wonder and delight.

To trust in the story of humanity is to see the inherent co-creation of the human experience. We are all souls, here to provide an experience for each other. The concepts of service and value are the keystones to the soul creating, in an untethered manner, through the human experience itself.

Our heart and soul are connected to all of humanity. The inspiration from our heart and soul always takes on the form of service to others. Our souls will attract other souls who take the form of the people who show up in our lives, fulfilling the agreed-upon soul contracts of this lifetime.

Those people who come into *your* life to assist you in fulfilling your life purpose are the people with whom *you* co-create the future. To witness and participate in each other's lives is the place of co-creation itself. To co-create is to amplify your ability to influence the collective kingdom, that collective paradigm that we experience as we are living out our lives interacting with each other, together.

To co-create with other souls who share similar visions provides the rocket fuel of creation. Where two or more have gathered, the creator itself shows up to co-create a new paradigm for humanity, a paradigm that comes through your heart. Inspired by your soul. You as an authentic genuine *you*. Living life exactly as you prefer.

Tune in to your own authentic self. Start with your heart. Slow your mind down and learn to distinguish when it is the one doing the talking. Purify your heart with the deep cleansers of forgiveness and compassion. Begin with yourself. As you purify your heart, you are able to capture a purer image of what is possible in your life, a human being fine tuning the authentic vibration of its own heart and soul, raising the core vibration of yourself. The human being who is so in tune with its own authentic nature knows intuitively, in each and every moment, the best path forward.

Those are the free souls who will pen a dream of tomorrow that generations to come will be talking about. It is the new frontier of our own personal sovereignty and expression, a true Citizen King, fulfilling the vision of tomorrow. You are here as a soul on this Earth with that as your potential.

May *your soul* fill you with the vision of an inspired life. May you know peace, prosperity and love. Dream your *best* dream. It is *your* soul inspiring *you*. Love You!

# ABOUT THE AUTHOR

Les Jensen began his lifework as an engineer in broadcast television, where he worked every day with high-power television transmitters. This hands-on experience with immense amounts of energy would later convey to him the language that he would ultimately use in his spiritual writings.

While moving through immense mental and emotional struggles in his life, Les discovered that vast amounts of energy were present within his subconscious, which he came to recognize as his own personal karma. While experiencing a life-changing and powerful event while in his mid-thirties, Les discovered how we store the immense power of karma within our own personal energy persona. Working with immense amounts of energy during his career provided him with an understanding of the language needed to explain the nature of one's personal power.

As he began to study the nature of his own personal power, Les discovered an ocean of unconditional love within his own heart. He learned how to bring himself into alignment with it, discovering that limitless power actually expands the more you use it, and realizing that power as love itself. He understood that this love has no boundaries, no limits.

As he worked with his own energy, clearing out that which did not promote his dreams coming true, Les discovered a purity located in the core of his being. He was then able to map the energetic nature of his human experience, which also translated to the same energetic nature found in all of humanity. After releasing his unresolved subconscious patterns that had bound this energy, Les discovered an inner light within himself, a light that had always been there, the light of love itself.

Over time, Les came to understand this inner light as the light and love of his very soul, a point of Divine love that had immense power to it. His soul had a purpose in mind for his life. It had an idea of what his ideal life would look like.

Les began to honor this inner life purpose. He started sharing this information with others so that they, too, could find their own inner light and set themselves free, living in this place of inner heaven while living out the human experience. Living from a place of authentic personal power. Living in the light. Living life fulfilled. Bringing Heaven to Earth and experiencing it—from the inside out.

In 2009, Les created New Human Living, a platform that promotes personal empowerment and Les' life purpose of being of service to others. He is also host of New Human Living Radio, where he enjoys insightful conversations with guests who are shaping the future of human consciousness.

Les' most recent book, *Personal Power Fundamentals*, reviews the fundamental nature of our own personal power, including how to overcome one's karmic propensities. Such a basic understanding can help students and people of all ages create more choices in their lives. This material is presented in an unbiased fashion, and is a great tool for anyone—including those involved in homeschooling and/or alternative curriculum courses—to grow a deeper understanding of their own personal power.

Les makes his home in Boulder, Colorado, USA, where he enjoys hiking, exploring the Rocky Mountains, and engaging others in passionate dialogue about the philosophy of our human nature.

To learn more, please visit NewHumanLiving.com and LesJensen.com.

Made in the USA
Middletown, DE
16 June 2018